ECHOING VOICES

ECHOING VOICES

*More Memories of a
Country House
Snooper*

JOHN HARRIS

JOHN MURRAY
Albemarle Street, London

First published in 2002
by John Murray (Publishers) Ltd.,
50 Albemarle Street, London W1S 4BD

A catalogue record for this book is available from the British Library

ISBN 0-7195-6483-2

Typeset in 11.5/14.5pt Bembo by Servis Filmsetting Ltd, Manchester
Printed and bound in Great Britain by
Butler & Tanner Ltd, Frome and London

To Tim Knox
Friend and Companion Snooper

Contents

Contents

Illustrations

Illustrations

ECHOING VOICES

Introduction

WE ALL SERVE an apprenticeship to life. Mine was fishing and the exploration of empty country houses with Uncle Sid, as related in *No Voice from the Hall*. Sid – or Snozzle – when not at West Worthing lived with Grandfather Harris on the southern edge of Uxbridge in Cowley Mill Road, so named after Rabb's Mill on the river Frays. Behind iron railings and red-and-black glazed brick supports the road bridge narrowed to a channel of swirling water frothed with white foam, to roar into a black hole under the mill. Little children hurried furtively past, always on the opposite pavement, because it was local lore that the 'Black Hole' had once swallowed a girl and spewed her out broken-limbed into the mill-race on the other side. The mill was set at an angle, and to the road were high walls. It had been burnt in 1898 and again in 1928, when milling ceased. But I can still see the tall chimney and the ubiquitous bulk of the nearby Gas Works. The mill was a barrier to what lay beyond, evoking from me the boyish refrain, 'But what's on the other side, Snozzle?' Sid had never fished the Frays 'on the other side', despite having been brought up nearby, with the upholstery workshop in the

1. Sid at Langley Park, Buckinghamshire, 1962

2. Cowley Mill or Rabb's Mill, Uxbridge, before the fire in
1928 (Uxbridge Local History Collection)

garden. Little could I have guessed in 1945 that more than half a
century later I would write about the 'other side', as I did in
Todd Longstaffe-Gowan's *London Gardener*, having identified it
as the garden and farm of John Rich, promoter and friend of
Hogarth, who painted a portrait of Rich's gardener here and
may even have advised on the garden layout. The tension of
anticipation was palpable when one day in May 1945 Sid met the
owner of Cowley Grove, once Rich's house but by then a
decayed boarding-house, the old stables a garage, and we
obtained permission to fish this stretch of the Frays. Even now I
can see Snozzle's red bulbous nose quivering at the prospect.

In fishing there is nothing better than to find virgin water. I
remember the reedy tench-filled canal behind the old Sanderson
wallpaper factory at the Uxbridge end of Denham; and the

Huntsmoor Park weir with the remains of the brick-walled gardens of the lost mansion of the Tower family; and an extra-ordinary rush-filled watercourse at one end of Denzlows Pits near Iver, from which more than twenty huge fat roach up to two pounds in weight were pulled in the course of one after-noon; and, in 1950, the trout streams in the state of Kedah in North Malaya that had seemingly never seen a fisherman.

So it was that Snozzle and I found ourselves on the 'other side'. Here was a brambly wilderness, the water still coursing around a man-made island in a Hogarthian, serpentine way. There were fragments of masonry, and the foundations of a bridge where the Frays was diverted into two channels. We could identify the bases of statues, long since removed but still shown on early Ordnance Survey maps, and the empty but dec-orative basin of an eighteenth-century fountain. Because it was channelled the water was fast, and in places surprisingly deep, and where it cut under the clayey banks, quieter pools were formed. Here the fat dace and roach seemed only too anxious to impale themselves on our hooks. By conflating these memories in my mind with what I later learned about Rich and Hogarth, I can now see that we were fishing in a decayed rococo garden. I can date this piscatorial foray accurately, for in June 1945 I left Greenway School, near the end of my thirteenth year.

As we cast our worms into the water, Sid spoke of my archae-ological aspirations. 'Can you make a living as an archaeologist?' he wondered out loud. 'Don't you need those things called degrees?' He was referring to our many sorties to look for flint axes in local gravel pits at West Drayton and Iver, or further afield at Taplow and Burnham, geologically known as the Higher and Lower Boyn Hill Terraces of the Thames. From Sid's bungalow at West Worthing we had scoured the South Downs, plotting the sites of flint mines on Blackpatch Hill. I was a budding prehistoric archaeologist keen to make my mark, like Edward Stevens of *Flint Chips* (1871) or A.D. Lacaille, whose article on 'The Palaeoliths from the Gravels of the Lower Boyn Hill Terrace around Maidenhead' (1940) I still possess, or V. Gordon Childe of *Man Makes Himself* (1941). I later discovered that even as we were fishing in Mr Rich's domain, Sid knew something I did not – that already I had been signed up by my father to be trained as an upholsterer at Messrs Heal and Sons in the Tottenham Court Road.

If I can isolate determining junctures in the passage of my life, one would be the 'Ruler' Mortlock incident, which gave me a distrust of formal education, another the Gamages Rebellion when, once I had discovered the Prehistoric Department of the British Museum with its hitherto undreamt-of possibilities, I determined to fend for myself, ignore parental wishes, and Not Be An Upholsterer. I enjoyed the companionship of the road in that halcyon time when car-owners were barred from youth hostels, and I suppose the peak of my drifting occurred between 1946 and 1949, three years during which I snooped about fifty empty houses. If not in a youth hostel, in summer I might sleep under the stars or in a church. Then came National Service, which taught me to be street-wise and provided a pathway through a till then uncertain future. Fooling the École du Louvre was part of that pathway. In retrospect I can see that my friendship with Richard Penard in Paris provided me with my first real mentor after Uncle Sid – a mentor of a very different sort, one who belonged to the world of collecting and connoisseurship, and who could afford it. By 1956 I could identify many more mentors: Francis Watson for connoisseurship (and for much else), Geoffrey Houghton Brown for taste in interior decor, Rupert Gunnis for collecting and antiquarianism, Howard

Colvin for probity and professionalism in architectural history, as well as an enthusiasm for British topography, and James Lees-Milne, my ideal of a catholic writer. These men made my early aspirations seem jejeune.

My fortuitous employment by the Royal Institute of British Architects in 1956 widened my *compagnonnage* to include all those who passed through the RIBA Library and Drawings Collection: Mark Girouard, Desmond Fitz-Gerald, Marcus Binney, even Henry Russell Hitchcock, became Companion Snoopers. Of course, when I married in 1960, Eileen brought into our orbit her own colleagues and friends, not least Rudolf Wittkower, Milton Lewine and Tony Clark. These American historians introduced me to connoisseurship in painting and sculpture, and Lewine and Clark in particular taught me that it was as important to buy art for one's personal enjoyment as to study it for academic enlightenment. Connoisseurship, the development of a critical faculty, was important to them, as it became to me: it was not enough to study art in museums, churches and private collections – the art trade must be scoured for discoveries. Architectural and art history, collecting and connoisseurship: the thrill of the chase embraced them all. But connoisseurship is unfashionable today, despised by many teaching departments. The 'New' art history and architectural history exclude it, and for architectural history this exclusion means a neglect of what is on the ground or in the field.

I have several times referred to what Ian Nairn called 'Pevsner Bashing'. For him this did not involve confrontational criticism of a great man, but rather a belief that Pevsner lacked that sense of quizzical intuition and enquiry necessary for a great topographer: he was incapable of reading a map creatively. And because he failed to wonder what was 'round the corner' or 'on the other side of the hill', he missed a great deal. For me, and for my

Companion Snoopers, when 'Pevsner Bashing' was uppermost in our minds it was as an incentive to look harder and search out as we snooped. The chase for what he missed has been a constant in my snooping since the appearance of *Middlesex* in the 'Buildings of England' series in 1951, and has added much excitement.

As an enthusiastic cartographer and map-reader I learned how to assault a country estate strategically, moving inwards from outlying estate farms and deer parks to the park wall itself, punctuated by gate lodges, then making the final but discreet assault on gardens and house. As recently as 1999 I was in a car with Nicky Haslam and other Companion Snoopers when we squealed to a halt in front of some locked park gates. Our unanimous outcry was, 'What is here?' It was in fact Hurstbourne Park in Hampshire, so we eagerly consulted *Hampshire* (Pevsner and Lloyd, 1967) and found the briefest of notes: James Wyatt's house for the Earl of Portsmouth *c.* 1780, burnt 1870, replaced by Beeston & Burmester 1894, demolished 1965. Not prepared to be defeated by shut gates, we hauled out the OS map and discovered a possible entry by means of a back drive. We passed some estate cottages, and the air filled with excited exclamations: 'What on earth is that cluster of Tudor chimneys sticking up romantically from behind that clump of trees? What of the vast walled kitchen gardens on our left – and on our left, too, aren't those Wyatt's stables?' Behind them was a nineteenth-century walled water garden – and in fact, the Beeston–Burmester house was all there bar one-third, and hideous it all was, utterly despoiled during and after the war. Whirling through the estate's Versailles-like avenues, we were warmed with satisfaction that Pevsner had missed so much.

I

'Ruler' Mortlock

MY MEMORY OF a rural Church of England school education
is of an accepted discipline. This I endured, and sometimes enjoyed, between 1936 and 1942, from the age of five to
eleven. Mr Harold Stoddart was headmaster, Mrs Waite head
teacher, Miss Mortlock assistant or under teacher. Religion and
patriotism reigned. At morning bell in the playground, to the
childish mind so vast but in reality small and confined, we would
line up as if in army platoons. Stoddart, Waite and Mortlock led
the parade, preceded by two favoured pupils, one carrying a
Union Jack, the other a church flag. We marched the short distance along the High Street to the church hall to hear school and
church announcements; on special days to receive some homily
from the vicar; and to sing patriotic songs of Empire – 'Some
talk of Alexander and some of Hercules'.

We all dreaded Miss Mortlock – a disciplinarian known as
'Ruler' Mortlock from her method of keeping order with a
ruler, administered on every possible occasion. Whispers in class
or excessive fidgeting would evoke the fearful summons –
'Nevard, stand forward' – and Nevard would step up to Miss

Mortlock at her rostrum, offer the right or left hand with fist clenched (or both hands, depending on the crime), to receive one crack or more on the knuckles with the ruler. So ingrained was our hatred of Mortlock that her death years later was a matter for whispered celebration.

Just before the 'Eleven-Plus' examination I was privileged, as a sign of accomplishment and expectation, to ring the morning bell. There was no doubt then but that I would pass to Bishopshalt Grammar School rather than the lowly Greenway School, and end up in a red-brick university. Later, in the last class of the day, we were versifying for 'Ruler' Mortlock. We had been reading Blake's 'Tyger Tyger, burning bright', and I adapted it to my own verse. Mortlock was horrified: I had *cheated*. This time it was not the ruler, but much worse. The command 'To the lavatories, Harris' was a dread one: it meant standing in the lavatory facing a urinal until called to the headmaster's study. So there I stood . . . and stood . . . and stood . . . until giggling boys came in after class, taunting that *they* were going home. Quiet descended. No one had called me to The Study. I poked my head out to a deserted school. I sidled towards the fearful Study. It too was deserted. What could I do but go home?

Next morning we assembled as usual, lined up in our platoons to march to the church hall. To my surprise, I was not allowed to ring the bell. In the church hall, without warning, I was called up onto the stage, where Stoddart announced that I had deliberately disobeyed a summons to his room, and would be caned. I was given no opportunity to explain that I had never been called from the lavatory. He was a brute. A swish on the right hand and a swish on the left, then I was ordered to bend over for a swish on the bum. From this point on I hated school, and deliberately failed the Eleven-Plus. However, the true culprit got his come-uppance for failing to order me in to see Stoddart, and for denying the fact. I belonged to the Cowley Gang, headed by Nevard: we cornered the blighter, fishing for tiddlers on the river Frays in Iver Lane, debagged him, and threw his clothes and shoes into the water with threats of 'Cops' and 'the Head'. Of course, in retrospect I can see that I owe much to that sneaky little fibber.

2

Dib, dib, dib and dob, dob, dob

G OD, KING AND Country – and of course the Boy Scouts –
went hand in hand at Cowley Church of England School.
A scout flag hung with the Union Jack in the church hall. In the
last few months of peace in the summer of 1939, trenches were
dug in Cowley Recreation Ground. We had to practise for an air
attack. At the sound of the sirens we assembled in the playground
and marched to the trenches. It's easy to imagine what Stukas
would have done had they been there to dive-bomb us. In 1942
we had a talk from a Chief Scout, exhorting us to 'do our bit'
by becoming cubs, scouts or guides. It was all very patriotic and
godly, with the parish priest taking school prayers twice a week.

In the main classroom hung a large map of the world on
which the Empire was coloured red. Geography was taken by
the headmaster Mr Stoddart, who would stand in front of the
map with his long pointer for a lesson in the naming of coun-
tries. He would shout 'Harris', or 'Nevard', or 'Fricker', and tap
a country. At this, up stood the designated boy to name it, and
gain a mark if he knew what was grown there. Even at that
tender age we sensed a certain futility in knowing where sisal

came from. Today we would probably retort 'Who cares a fuck?' – but then we did not know what 'fuck' meant. Adrian Nevard was sent to the corner for taking the micky: 'Sir, why is our Empire coloured red? Does it mean our soldiers lost lots of blood?'

Adrian, David Fricker, Derek Jarman and I joined the Scouts together, but not for long. The tying of knots seemed daft, as also the 'dib, dib, dib' and 'dob, dob, dob' nonsense, and songs around the camp fires – 'We're riding along on the crest of the wave, and the sun is in our eyes'. Our introduction to scouting was positively Freudian. Newly kitted-out, we first met one autumnal evening in the old brickfield orchards for indoctrination into Scout lore. To us the Scoutmaster of the Cowley Troop seemed a grown man, but I suppose in truth he was little more than a gangling adolescent. When the camp fire had died down and the bottles of Tizer were empty, in the shadowy gloaming he gathered his recruits around him. We were to be introduced to what was called 'Penny and Tuppence': 'For a penny I'll show it to you' (opening his flies) 'and for tuppence you can hold it.' Jarman always had more money than the rest of us, and he felt it, withdrawing his hand as if it were hot. Perhaps it was. No one asked whether there was anything on offer 'for thruppence'.

We were very naïve. Not long after this initiation ceremony we found a mysterious deflated-looking rubbery thing with a knob at the end, creamy in colour, lying in the gutter on Iver Lane, Cowley. Adrian picked it up. 'What is it?' he quizzed. 'Someone's balloon,' we all answered, and Adrian put it to his mouth to blow it up.

3

The room at the top of the stairs

THE WOOD YARD belonging to W.S. Try, Builders, in Cowley, Middlesex, was a playground for 'the Cowley Gang', who were all at Greenway Elementary School. Adrian Nevard was the son of the manager of this building firm, and my miscreant pal. The yard extended from Cowley High Street to the river Frays on its western boundary and comprised a cottage where the Try family lived, stores, the paint and carpenters' shops, and open canopied sheds to store timber. These last were a magnet for little boys playing cowboys and indians, soldiers, Hitler SS, or bandits. We split up into gangs of baddies and goodies, and hid behind piles of wood with pop-guns to shoot or ambush the enemy. Sometimes we took planks of wood to the river and made rafts.

Once Adrian and I were alone there. We had taken the yard's boat from the jetty to row up and down the Frays – but we were bored. We wanted excitement of a different sort. Adrian decided to climb into the paint shop through a window. He had been there with his father a week earlier, and had lifted off a window-catch undetected. We climbed in. What exciting oily smells! The shop was of the old-fashioned sort, there since Try's was founded in the nineteenth century. It was built of black, tarred wood, with long stretches of window. We opened pots of paint, stuck our fingers in, stirred with sticks, mixed colours. Adrian grew bolder and drew a love heart on a window pane: 'Brenda Buttram [who was my next-door neighbour in Clammas Way] loves A. Nevard.'

We noticed a short flight of steps rising to a locked door. What was there, we wondered? Adrian had an idea. The lock was conventional, and there were many like it elsewhere in the shops. He scuttled away. Sure enough, another key fitted. There was mounting excitement as the door opened onto a room no more than eight feet square with a single small window. It contained a pile of suitcases, several trunks, an officer's sword, and trench-coats hung on pegs. Later it occurred to me that those were the effects of a Try subaltern killed in the First World War. I never asked, because of what happened next.

For two naughty boys the opening of those trunks was sheer delight, as we revelled in the possibilities of the unknown. Adrian pulled out a large and expensive Swiss knife, the sort with many blades and uses. He put it in his pocket. Then he found a Colt revolver in a belt-case. The thrill induced an awed silence in both of us. Now we could be *real* soldiers, and attack the German hordes in the timber sheds. He pointed it at me, and pulled the trigger. It went click. 'Hurry, let's hide it,' I said. Our pals would be so impressed when we brought it out. Adrian shouted 'Boom! Boom!', extended his arm in my direction, and pulled the trigger again. There was an enormous explosion, the gun was flung up and out of his hand, and the bullet went straight through the roof. The noise terrified us, and the room reeked of gunpowder. Surely the whole world must have heard? The police would arrive to the sound of sirens. We would go to prison. Very frightened, Adrian shoved the gun into the trunk and we fled, back out through the paint shop window, down to the river where we waded across to the fields on the other side, and ran pantingly along the towpath of the Grand Union Canal. Then we dived down a gulley, and were out of sight by the Hunziker brick factory where we had our secret camp.

We were never taken to task about the gun. The Try painters found the window open and Adrian's love note on the glass, but if the bullet-hole was noticed, nothing was said. He got a severe ticking-off, and Try's yards were put out-of-bounds. But that was not the end of the story: that came one snowy winter in Cowley Recreation Ground. Adrian was proud of his Swiss knife, and that day he was dropping it from a height, to cut snowballs in two on the ground. Then it dropped onto the back of my hand. Red blood spurted on white snow. I badly needed stitches, but my parents never liked doctors. The gash was allowed not only to mend badly but to become infected. The doctor at the hospital was suspicious of the deep knife-like cut, and of my explanation that I had unwisely put my hand underneath the runners while tobogganing, and it must have been cut by some glass.

The revolver and the knife passed into Cowley legend. It was not long before rumours spread about Russian roulette, and the bullet across the hand. I felt very proud. A few months later I was wondering whether maybe I had been saved for something I could not as yet fathom.

4

Fire! Fire!

Brandon Park, Suffolk

A T 28 CLAMMAS Way in Cowley we had one of Sir John Anderson's shelters in the middle of the potato and cabbage patch. It did not matter that water dripped through the turfed roof, or that no oil heater could get rid of the rheumatic damp. To a nine-year-old it was an ancient earthwork, or maybe a Viking warrior's grave. I mythologized about an ancient incursion up the Thames and a great battle around Langley Park – hence the iron javelins in the country-house museum there. Uncle Sid had already introduced me to the gravel pits of West Drayton, and above my wooden Anderson bunk I reverently laid the flint axes we found there on a shelf. I have them still, at Badminton. War was fun.

My father and mother, Fred and Maud, suffered from the aching damp of the shelter, so when father became a fire-watcher at South Kensington, mother moved back into the house, sleeping beneath the stairs. One night the fairy lights of a cluster of incendiary bombs lit up the garden. We boldly pulled back the curtains of the back room to watch the pretty 'fire-works' that eventually fizzled out and were collected in a bucket

3. Flint axes from the gravel pits at Iver, Buckinghamshire,
found with Uncle Sid in 1940

by air-raid wardens. I got used to the thumping and crumping,
and later to the chug chug of V-1s, yearning in my childish way
for the exhaust light to go out, when it would dive to earth.
Once one did, and laid waste to a few bungalows and a few lives
at the end of Clammas Way.

Then Herbert Morrison stepped in with *his* shelter, an iron
room–within–a–room – or rather, an iron and steel mesh-encased
bed. I would pull the curtains to and imagine the house collaps-
ing, with me snug and safe in my iron tomb. It was a boy's
delight, for the Hornby train set could be laid out on its top, the
size of a double bed. (Years later, in the garden of Oxton Hall in

4. Flint-flaking at Brandon, Suffolk: descendants of the prehistoric flakers in Grimes Graves

Nottinghamshire, demolished in 1957, I saw a Morrison Shelter,
complete with its wire-mesh protection, being used as a chicken
run.) When the unpredictable V-2s began to descend, however,
it was considered time for thirteen-year-old Johnny Harris to
spend a few peaceful months 'evacuated' to Brandon in Suffolk.
It was August 1944, according to the cancellation on a postcard
titled 'Flaking Flints, Brandon'.

A relative of my mother's brother Bill Sellwood worked for
the Forestry Commission, who had bought the Brandon estate
from Lord Wigan's widow in 1936. Today, with the house and
its mausoleum, it is marked on the Ordnance Survey map as
Brandon Country Park, a mile south of Brandon, and west of
the Elveden Road. *Paterson's Roads* informs me that Edward Bliss

5. The Bliss Mausoleum, Brandon, Suffolk

lived here in the early nineteenth century. He bought the estate in 1820 and built a new house in 1826. The white Regency style is what I remember and a recent visit confirms it, suggesting that this severe-looking house with two Paestum Doric porticoes might have been designed by W.J. Donthorne, who worked extensively in East Anglia. A treat was to skirt the lake, plunge into a brambly wood and discover the spiky Gothic brick mausoleum built for Mr Bliss, who died in 1845. The door could be pulled open to reveal, in the light filtering in from dirty windows, a recess in each wall, one for the coffin of Mr Bliss, the other for his wife's. I would hurriedly shut the door with a cry and run for safety, but I returned again and again for another thrill. Pevsner missed Brandon Park in 1961, as did his reviser in 1974.

At Liverpool Street I was put on an LNER (London and North-East Railways) train with a bag, my fishing rod and tackle, and a large label instructing me to change at Cambridge, where a smaller smelly Thomas the Tank Engine train took me by way of Ely to Brandon. It was my first experience of the Fens. I counted the stops from Ely: Shippea Hill, Lakenheath and then Brandon. I cannot now disinter from my memory the name of my temporary 'parents', so I shall call them Mr and Mrs Forester. I recollect Mrs Forester on the platform, with a peculiar long face and teeth an orthodontist should have attended to. I don't recall ever seeing her without her green apron. Their Garage Flat was in offices or stables at Brandon Park, and has recently been demolished to make way for an extension to the house, which is now a nursing home.

Uncle Sid had already extolled the fishing at Brandon: the Little Ouse from Lakenheath to Thetford was celebrated in fishy annals. I was gobbling with excitement the first time I leaned over the late medieval Brandon Bridge, in Town Street, to look down onto the crystal clear waters. How I yearned for Uncle Sid! Dozens of fat roach swayed with the weeds, and I could spy eels performing their sinuous ballet in the lower depths. I fished every day and caught at least thirty roach weighing up to one and a half pounds each, a good two-pound perch, and many eels. They were all returned except for the eels, which the Foresters enjoyed. They made a change from dried-egg powder. I remember Mrs Forester telling me with a shiver that a previous owner of the house had collected human skulls, and recently I have sorted this out: Henry Aldridge, a nephew of Edward Bliss, inherited Brandon in 1845, the Portugese title of Baron Alreyo in 1855 and the Spanish estates and title of Barton Baretto in 1869. It was his son, Henry d'Alreyo, who collected human skulls, when he lived at Brandon between 1890 and 1903.

I walked one day to Weeting, just over the border in Norfolk. Weeting Hall was in American occupation, and I remember American troops who were very friendly: 'Waan some gum, chum?' There seemed to be a city of Nissen huts. The Hall was demolished in 1952, and I can imagine the nasty modern housing estate which followed. I found a ruined church and castle, but far more exciting was an ancient steam tractor, its brass, copper and green enamel surface decorations all dulled, its great wheels sinking into the sandy earth, just like an abandoned dinosaur. Uncle Sid had implored me to visit the prehistoric flint mines of Grimes Graves (now an English Heritage site), but the caves had been closed since the final days of the 1939 excavation season that preceded the war. Flint knapping had been an industry around Brandon for thousands of years, long before knapped flint was used in the building of medieval churches, or to provide the spark to ignite the powder in old-fashioned guns.

I think this was when I experienced my first encounter with an empty house, Thetford Warren Lodge, a fifteenth-century flint tower near Thetford, just off the Brandon–Thetford road. Mr Forester took me one afternoon to the Lodge, parked his truck, and left me for an hour. I remember only dirt and dust, and some evidence of fire, and have no precise memory of any architectural detail. But as I sat by a fir tree, my hand made contact with something hard and cold, and from the dirt and the fir cones I lifted out a perfect flint knapped dagger about nine inches long. This was better than all the fish in the Ouse! Eventually I gave it to the British Museum, where it was declared to be Danish. Years later, regretting this gift, I asked to see it again. The Museum had mislaid it!

Looking back, the relevance of all the ominous notices in red lettering warning people to 'Keep Out' seems clear. Miles of impenetrable barbed-wire fences divided the warrens, and the US Army seemed to be everywhere. I now suspect that Mr Forester, although he was apparently employed by the Americans in some capacity, was not entirely aware that hereabouts, dispersed in hiding-places across the many square miles of forest, was one of the largest ammunition dumps in Britain.

One evening towards the end of August the sound of fire engine sirens was heard constantly for some hours. Mr Forester did not come home. In the middle of the night I was aroused from sleep by Mrs Forester and told of forest fires close to Brandon Park: I must quickly dress. I remember acrid smoke hanging in the air, and the reflections of flames on the near horizon. Fire engines raced along the Elveden road, and three lorries were removing residents. I was bundled aboard and we drove westwards, I am told towards Ely. The US Army had provided tents, and lovely food of a sort not tasted since war had begun. What more could a thirteen-year-old desire in the way of excitement? But maybe I would have thought differently if I had known that half of Suffolk was in danger of blowing up, should the Brandon fires reach the dumps. The potential disaster was a well-kept secret, but the fire itself was too much for my parents in Cowley. My father met me on the platform at Ely, and I was swept back under parental supervision.

5

The Gamages rebellion

AMONG MY EARLIEST memories of 28 Clammas Way in Cowley is of a tiresome family routine. Every other Saturday my parents would make a shopping expedition to Gamages, that middle-class department store in High Holborn. The expedition was preceded by bustling preparations, scrubbing, starching and polishing. How I yearned for those alternate free Saturdays.

We would walk the dreaded school route through Cowley (with fearful glances from me at the Church of England school) to the bus stop at Iver Lane and the High Street, for the red number 222 from West Drayton, or the green 458 from Slough via Iver. Both drew in to Uxbridge bus station at the rear of what I later recognized as Holden's fine concrete modern Metropolitan and Piccadilly Line terminus. Even then I was aware of the contrast between it and the friendly Georgian-columned Market House opposite. Generally we took the Piccadilly Line direct to Holborn, but if the Metropolitan Line train was first out we changed to the Piccadilly Line at Rayners Lane. I later learned from relatives that this monotonous routine

6. Gamages, Holborn

began in 1933, when I was two, so by 1939, when I was eight, in that summer before the Hitler War, I must have visited Gamages more than a hundred times. It was purgatory, for I soon tired of watching the pneumatic till system, which whooshed the invoice and the customer's money away in a brown-metal and brass tube-like container, and whooshed any change and a receipt back again.

Gamages would be followed by a visit to the Sellwood family, my mother's relations, who lived at Cliff Villas by the old Caledonian Market. The house is there still. Twelve sisters and a brother had been brought up in this end-of-terrace house next to a school and facing old turf-embanked reservoirs which were built over (a block of flats) in the 1930s. By 1939 a *frisson* went through Cliff Villas whenever we arrived, due solely to my rebellious behaviour. Over the years I broke up the toilet bowl with a hammer; let loose six white mice (bought in the Market) in the 'best' front room, to frighten aunts Cissie, Aggie, and

Gladdie; and melted brown boot polish into the large bowl of dripping that always stood on the table in the kitchen, where bread and dripping was a staple.

The futility of this fortnightly expedition was underlined by my father's daily routine: at 6.35 every weekday morning he bicycled from Cowley to Uxbridge to catch the 7.02 Piccadilly Line train to South Kensington and the upholstery workshops of Percy Bass. To more or less repeat this every other Saturday seemed, as I later moaned to Uncle Sid, 'just plain daft'.

Then came The War. For four years I watched incendiary bombs dropping in our garden and doodlebugs chugging across the sky. Children of that age – eight to thirteen – are uncomprehending of death. I yearned for black-booted Gestapo to come surging across the Maygoods Farm Brick Field that bounded our rear garden, where I did sentry duty with a pop-gun and catapult outside the Anderson shelter. But more than anything, the war meant deliverance from Gamages. I prayed every night for it to be blown up.

At the age of thirteen I was looking forward to my last year at the Greenway School, Uxbridge. Soon I would walk the mile and a bit by the Great Western Railway branch line from Cowley to Uxbridge for the last time: no mamby-pamby school buses in those days. D-Day was announced, and as I ate my boiled egg with soldier's fingers mum commented, 'It'll be lovely to go up to Gamages again.' I think one soldier's finger hovered unregarded in my open mouth at that pregnant remark. VE day arrived, and Mr Wilgoose of Greenway organized a 'chara' up to London for the celebrations. All I remember, above the crowds and the singing, was mother saying 'Fred, find out when Gamages are re-opening.'

I had thought this dreaded excursion was behind me. My weekends now were spent fishing with Uncle Sid and looking for flint implements in gravel pits. But reinstated the routine was, although now we had moved (as we didn't say then) 'up market': no longer Gamages, but Heal's. The reason for the change was revealed towards the end of June 1945, when I bade my thankful farewell to Greenway school. On that last walk home I may well have gone tiddling, as I routinely did, in the Low and Shawyers brook. I sensed tension upon arriving home, but went upstairs to my room to lay out my Acheulean flint implements on the bed, as I routinely did − I must by then have collected more than fifty − and formulate thoughtful adolescent conclusions. I was summoned to supper. Mum and Dad were glancing at one another, and I was surprised to see two of my father's tack-hammers laid on the table. 'What on earth for?' I wondered. With a choking pride in his voice, Dad announced that I had been accepted to train as an upholsterer at Heal's. I would start in July. Generations of my family had been upholsterers, and that I would follow them was neither questioned, nor indeed put to the vote. I had planned to spend the summer searching in some new gravel workings near Burnham Beeches. It was a terrible blow.

I remember two further Saturday trips. One was to Heal's, to be shown around; the other was supposed to be to Cliff Villas, but I never arrived there. In those days the automatic closing doors on the Piccadilly and Metropolitan Line trains were an innovation. My ghoulish juvenile mind yearned for them to close on a neck and chop the head off, to roll bloodily on the slatted wooden floors: head, hands, feet − it did not matter which. I enjoyed imagining people I disliked suffering this fate (even today I have a yearning for someone to not 'Mind the gap', but fall down it).

That day I cracked. Damn Heal's, damn Gamages, damn Cliff Villas. At Ickenham and Swakeleys station, the third stop out of

Uxbridge, just as the doors were about to close, I leapt up and flung myself out of the carriage. I was free on the platform, as Mother and Father stared in horrified disbelief through the train window. I laughed. This was the cutting of the umbilical cord. The train pulled out, and suddenly I felt lonely, standing on the platform. I must return to Clammas Way to fortify the house against all-comers. My private war had begun.

I closed all the windows, pulled the curtains, bolted all the doors, turned the keys in all the locks. With satisfaction I surveyed the food in the pantry. I fantasized: after this, they would never return. They would stay in Cliff Villas. I could educate myself on the *Encyclopaedia Britannica*, kept in its glazed cupboard in the front room. Alas for childish dreams! Reality was harsh. They returned by the next train. Hardly had I finished fortifying my castle when there came the sound of a key in a door that would not open. Then Mum shouted, 'John, open up! Don't be silly.' My refusal led to much knocking and banging, then a pause, then more pleading, and threats of a beating. I remained silent. Through the letter box I heard, 'I'll whip you!' Then another pause, and Mr and Mrs Buttrum from next door joined in the fray.

A tinkle of broken glass signalled a determined parental assault, followed by a shattering of glass when my father's hand, in trying to open the inside latch of the kitchen window, knocked over a glass bowl. I was for it. I retreated to the back garden room. Father was now behind the inner kitchen door, shouting that he'd break it down and thrash my bottom. I pulled the curtains aside and peered down the garden. Seeing no 'enemies', I quickly climbed out through the metal Crittal windows and dashed to the hole in the hedge that led to the Maygoods Farm Brick Field.

I crossed to the Apple Orchards to consider my situation. I had two sixpences in my pocket. Beyond the orchard was the branch line of the Great Western Railway from West Drayton to Uxbridge, and a footpath to Cowley station. I must seek refuge with Sid. I bought a single ticket to Uxbridge and caught the lovely smelly, steamy, tank-engine-drawn train. From Uxbridge station I followed the footpath along the river Frays to the sanctuary of my bachelor uncle, my fishing companion. 'Ooooo!' he said, his huge conk reddening. 'You're in for it.' His face wrinkled up with laughter. 'Mind you, I never could understand those terrible trips to Gamages.' He went into the next room to phone my parents. All I could hear was the muffled sounds of his end of a very long conversation. He came back. 'You can stay here. They'll calm down – but as for Heal's, well, we'll have to see how things go.' My lode star from now on was Uncle Sid, who encouraged me to follow my own inclinations, come what might.

6

Not to be an upholsterer

Heal's

THE DAY OF the reluctant upholsterer began with the necessity of catching the 6.52 Metropolitan Line train from Uxbridge to Euston Square. Arriving at Heal's in the Tottenham Court Road by 7.55 on my first morning in July 1945 I was revolted by the constraint of 'clocking in', the punch and ting of the surveillance of time. In my bag I had my father's venerated tack-hammers (I have them still, and use them). As I entered the upholsterers' shop for the first time, I could hardly breathe. I wanted to turn round and run away. Through the length of the 'Shop' were chairs and settees set up on trestles, each pair of which marked the perimeter of one upholsterer's work area. I need not dwell on my discontent. I was met by Mr Gillett, the friendly shop foreman, his status marked by a long beige coat. Tea breaks were judged by the second. The 'dinner' break came not fifty seconds before, nor fifty seconds after, but precisely at one o'clock. The conversation was inane.

Nothing could have been more discouraging. I took to disappearing on forays of exploration through the store and workshops, and found the perfect hideaway. Furniture awaiting

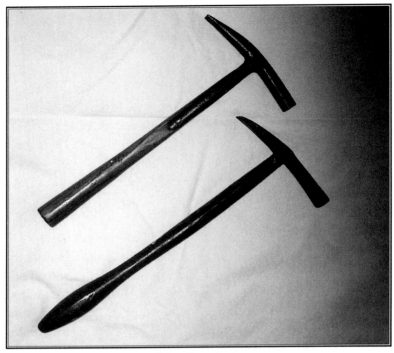

7. My father's tack-hammers

upholstery was stored outside the workshop in a gloomy, low-ceilinged space, filled with two levels of timber flooring or supports, where there was a glazed light at floor level, and a tantalizing door not three feet square. This gave onto a service passage full of gurgling water pipes, and, where the pipes turned into the vertical, opened into another passage with two steps up to a 'secret room' above the upholstery shop (only later did I discover the location of its door, which was padlocked on the outside). To me it was The Room That Heal's Forgot. Stacked up were rolls of red, green, blue and yellow parachute silk, left-overs from the Parachute Manufacturers' Association, which had been here from 1943 to 1945. I would wrap them around myself and re-live the exploits of 'Pasha' Harris, serving under Kitchener in the Sudan.

During my time at Heal's I kept a little store of books here, mostly about flints, including Batsford's *Everyday Life in the New Stone, Bronze and Early Iron Age*. There was also some poetry. It surprises me today to think that I was reading Eliot and Auden. This silk room was my bolt-hole. Three times I stayed overnight, after stocking up with grub and a bottle of Tizer. I would clock off, and then 'forget' something and rush back inside, hoping the gate man, the spy of all comings and goings, would not notice my failure to return.

Within two weeks of starting at Heal's I had discovered the British Museum and its flint collection, and soon I was there every lunch time, having volunteered to help sort flint implements in the Prehistoric Department. I always returned late. There were no illusions in the upholstery shop, or on the part of the foreman, as to my potential as an upholsterer. Then one day the gate man put his hand on my shoulder and said, 'We've been watching you. You're wanted.' I was taken up to the Management, sacked, and told to remove my personal belongings. This meant a last crawl through the passage into my den to retrieve my books, and as a momento I took a square of red silk. I still have it. My parents were mortified, and I can now understand their deep sense of grievance. But I also remember the intense pleasure of clocking off for the last time. Under the gate man's nose, I vigorously punched the card a dozen times, then tore it into little pieces and threw the pieces at him.

I marched out into the sunlight of Tottenham Court Road. For a long while to come the tyranny of the time-clock gave way to flints, fishing, youth hostels, hitch-hiking, and Uncle Sid. There were interludes of work, of course: at Astor Boissilier and

Lawrence at West Drayton I tested waxes in their laboratory, and each Thursday skived off to the nearby gravel pits instead of learning science at Ealing Technical College. I was soon sacked. There was also an interval at Richmond Technical College, when I shared a room by Kew Gardens with a rich Calcutta merchant's son who died tragically on holiday, of rabies. I was due to start my National Service in December 1949, and was almost longing for it to begin. At least there would be some certainty about the immediate future.

7

To Malaya

MY BASIC TRAINING in the Royal Army Medical Corps at Crookham Barracks, near Fleet in Hampshire, has already been alluded to in 'A Polish patriot's place: Dogmersfield Park', in *No Voice from the Hall*. I would skive off into the surrounding country at every opportunity. Then 22318793 Acting Lance Corporal Harris was ordered to study hygiene and sanitation. My posting to the Army School of Hygiene at Mychett in Hampshire, in March 1950, extended the range of my forays after empty country houses, although many then, so near Aldershot, were still in military occupation. I excelled only in the history of malaria: my paper on the hygiene of cook-houses received two marks out of ten. The pleasant six weeks I spent at Mychett were put to more effective use, I thought, with the aid of my OS map: Farnborough was at hand, and Elvetham Park, Henley Park, and a J.B. Papworth house at Hartley Witney, and so many others in this part of north Hampshire, all beckoning with their siren calls.

My absences did not go unremarked. I had been AWOL – absent without leave – five times, each offence confining me to barracks and to the performance of menial tasks. I was sure to be given the worst possible posting once the course was completed. Twelve of us were duly summoned to stand in line, waiting to be called in to receive our posting. The feared voice of Staff-Sergeant Daly booms at a gloomy Harris: 'Commanding Officer's interview – 'ten-shun!' I march in. The officer looks up. 'Stand at ease, Harris. High marks for initiative, low marks for hygiene studies. You have been absent without leave five times,' he continued. 'What are these country houses you see?' I had been late returning from Dogmersfield Park, and late again from discovering Waverley Abbey, and even later when, after intruding into the decayed Victorian kitchen gardens of Heckfield Place, I took tea unexpectedly with Lord Brocket at Bramshill Park. I explained my interest.

To my surprise, I was offered a choice of three Hygiene Assistant Grade 3 posts in the rank of Corporal/Sergeant: Bermuda, Trieste or Malaya. During that brief interview I ruminated for a few seconds: Trieste I could see any time; Bermuda seemed somehow too sybaritic; so Malaya it would be.

Fate was smiling when the clapped-out *Empire Windrush* broke down in Colombo for three days. With the connivance of a friendly merchant seaman, my 'Uncle Reginald, tea-planter' phoned the ship to ask if his 'nephew' Corporal Harris might be allowed shore leave. I was. Having already become a member of the Royal Asiatic Society, I promptly made for the National Museum. It was closed. Even today I marvel at my impertinence in asking the gate-lodge keeper to telephone the director to come and show me his museum. He did so, and then he and his wife took me to their cottage in Kandy. Here I promptly caught a form of dengue; immediately I arrived in Singapore I was hospitalized, and so missed the horrible postings to encampments in the *ulu*, the jungles of Perak, which fell to my four unfortunate RAMC Hygiene Assistant companions on the *Empire Windrush*.

My lot was to be sent up-country to HQ RAMC Kuala Lumpur, and it was here that Fate again took my side. I was interviewed by Colonel D'Arcy, Commanding Officer of RAMC Malaya, for a posting to Sungei Patani in Kedah, North Malaya. When he asked about my 'hobbies', I replied 'archaeology', and told him I had joined the Malayan Branch of the Royal Asiatic Society. 'Then I'll send you to see Major Peter Williams-Hunt. Archaeologist chap. Advisor on Aborigines,' said D'Arcy (this was the time of the Communist insurgency in Malaya). I remember a small office with lots of maps on the wall, a moustachioed man of infectious enthusiasm dressed not in standard jungle green but partly in native costume. He somehow had the impression that I was a graduate of the Institute of Archaeology in Regent's Park: I did not disillusion him. He told me a great deal about the archaeology of Northern Malaya, indicated on a map where I would find 'middens', or habitation sites, on the sea coast near Sungei Patani, and later took me to visit caves in the mountainous area of Grik, where there was evidence of early habitation hearths in the guano or bats' droppings that had accumulated over a thousand years. Neither then nor later did he mention that he was married to Wa Dramman, a beautiful daughter of a Semai Senoi aboriginal headman. It's not hard to imagine what his stuffy Colonial contemporaries would have made of that. Myths have been woven around Williams-Hunt, of which the only verified fact is his horrible death, falling into a pig-trap onto poisoned stakes. But by then I had left Malaya with my oily reputation.

8

The oiling of the waters

I MAGINE THE SCENE: geographically, we are in Sungei Patani in the state of Kedah, North Malaya. The date is May 1950, the building a wooden hygiene office belonging to a Casualty Clearing Station of the Royal Army Medical Corps, at a military camp then occupied by a Gurkha regiment. My veranda looks out over an old RAF airfield, still the graveyard of grassed-in skeletons of Brewster Buffaloes, shot up on the ground by the Japs' efficient Zeros in December 1941.

Such were my quarters as National Serviceman 22318793 Harris, now a sergeant and a Hygiene Assistant Class III. My predecessor Jim Wilkins, known as Whippet Wilkins for his narrow long face, had been a Regular, and when demobbed in Penang as a sergeant he took up with a Liverpudlian rubber planter known as Scouse Scorer, of dubious reputation – I met both of them in the course of the next few months. They bought two fishing boats and rented a small remote island off the coast north of Alor Star, the capital of Kedah. With their desirable Siamese girl friends they provided many services, some of which attracted the attentions of the Malayan Police.

I must now return to the veranda, which at the cool hour of five in the morning was a scene of bustling activity. Chee Chin Chong, my Straits Chinese civilian overseer, would be supervising the line-up of ten Tamil oilers, each with a tank of kerosene on his back and a sprayer in his hand. They were to carry out the daily ritual of oiling the waters, in order to destroy the breeding larvae of the dreaded anophelese mosquitoes that spread malaria. I was a novice in all this. Upon my arrival from Singapore and Kuala Lumpur Chong had handed me an inventory to sign, for the stores. 'No need to check,' he reassured me. 'Sergeant Wilkins kept good accounts.' I signed. Little did I know.

Three weeks passed, and Chong presented me with the month's indent for 1,500 gallons of kerosene. Once again I innocently signed. At the following morning's dawn parade, which I was now in the habit of taking languidly from the comfort of my rattan chair, I noticed the legend '4 gallons' impressed in the metal of one Tamil's army-issue tank. Head on one side, I exercised my mental arithmetic: four gallons per Tamil, ten Tamils, oiling for twenty-eight days – that surely made 1,120 gallons? I hurried to the indent files. All was revealed. There were indents dating back to October 1948, signed by the Whippet, all for 1,500 gallons a month, 380 more than were actually used. At that rate, more than seven thousand gallons had been spirited away.

'Chong, come here,' I called, and firmly shut the office door, over which I had already put up my personal sign, 'CORDON SANITAIRE'. 'Where, Chong, have 7,220 gallons of kerosene gone to?' I looked into his inscrutable moustachioed face. 'Now, come clean.' I got a big smile, and an admission: 'The Sungei Patani Department of Public Health take it off us.' Chong explained that the employer of the Tamils was none other than the Works Commissioner who managed the accounts. He took his cut, as did the Whippet, as did Chong, who of his bounteous generosity gave each oiler a few dollars for his co-operation and housekeeping. 'My God!' I expostulated. 'We'll all go to gaol!' This earned me another beatific smile, and also a cautionary, loaded comment: 'We might all disappear. Whippet Wilson now has many friends. Don't worry,' Chong added. 'It's all now much easier. Being on Active Service means no one checks.' He then told me that, incredibly, the number of oilers had been reduced in 1948 – but the military was still paying for the original complement. He was right. When every month a fat wodge of dollars was put into my hand, what could I do but open an account at the Chartered Bank of India, Australia and China, where the cheques were very prettily printed? Chong had of course to inform the Whippet that I knew. I will say only that 'mum was the word', for him as well as me. I was like that First World War song, 'The bells of hell go ting-a-ling-a-ling for you as well as me'. He knew the score as well as I did, and I took advantage of his offer of weekends on Pulau Bentong with his pretty Siamese consorts.

I always had a nagging fear that someone, sometime, would check the paperwork. No one ever did. I had made eighteen bank deposits when one day I looked up to see my command-ing officer framed in my doorway. 'No more oiling,' he said, waving a paper. 'It's now the job of the Department of Public Health. We're to give them our equipment, and any surplus oil.' Chong was mortified. When my time in Malaya was up and my travel warrant came through for the long train journey to Singapore and the troopship to Blighty, I took all the indent papers to the incinerator. All evidence of those Tamil oilers who had been absent without leave for the past four years went up in smoke.

9

The Harbour Master's mistake

In Easter 1951 I roared into Alor Star station on my BSA 350, on leave and free from army discipline for five days. Everything about me was improper: I was on active service, but with my passport ready to cross frontiers illegally; I was dressed in civilian clothes on an army motor-bike; I was carrying my army revolver in a bag. My destination was Sukhothai (I think I called it Singora then) in Siam, now Thailand, with its Buddhist monasteries and its giant standing Buddhas. The preceding Christmas I had taken seven days' illicit leave and flown from Penang to Bangkok and on to Phnom Penh to see the temples of Angkor Wat. Then, as this Easter, I was officially enjoying the flesh-pots of Penang, that beautiful island where most military personnel took their leave. I now had an hour to wait for my train – but, alas, the station master reported the line blown up at Mata Ayer, on the Malayan side of the border. No hope of another train for three days.

What should I do? I left the bike in a hotel car park, and leaned contemplatively against the bar with a Tiger beer. A Straits Chinaman was drinking too, and we exchanged greetings. He was the Harbour Master. I explained my dilemma, mentioning the RAMC but not my rank. 'Why not go to Pulau Langkawi?' he suggested. 'Group of islands. Night's trip. Lovely place. Rest house called the Sanatorium, owned by the Sultan of Kedah. A party's leaving this evening. Boat returns for you in four days. I'll ring the harbour office.' I could hardly refuse. I was brought up short when I heard him say, 'It's a Captain Harris, RAMC. He'll be along in half a hour.'

Early that evening found me on a large motorized junk piled with boxes and packages, dozens of crates of beer, netted bags of vegetables, wooden pens with squarking fowl, and three bicycles. I introduced myself to two French planters from a Kedah rubber estate – a couple of tough gays – the elderly wife of the manager of a tin mine who was already on the island, and a Colonial civil servant named Peter Bissell. I pinked a little when they welcomed 'Captain Harris'. We passed the old ruined fort on the Kedah River and chugged out on a darkening sea, the sky streaked in a technicolour of vivid reds, blues, mauves and oranges. The French planters were soon drunk on whisky. They had been ambushed three times by Communist bandits, and were planning to return to Algeria. Uptight Mr Bissell said not a word. Mrs Tin Mine chattered nothings. She had been here before the Japanese invasion, had returned in 1948, and was opposed to Malay independence. She kept asking me probing medical questions, to which I responded that I was in charge of anti-malaria operations – which of course I was, with my Tamil oilers at Sungei Patani.

The junk hissed softly across smooth moonlit waters. I slept curled up on the deck until a suffusing golden sunrise revealed a conical green mountain on the horizon; this was Mount Raya, reputedly an extinct volcano. Langkawi was about twenty-five miles across, fringed with a necklace of more than twenty other brilliant emerald green islands each set in a collar of gold sand, and all uninhabited. We tied up at the only pier, just below the rest house. A portly, Blimpish husband welcomed Mrs Tin. The two inebriated planters wobbled their way up to the rest house where a Malay servant in whites, red *bandang* and round black cap extended a helping hand. Surprisingly, Mr Bissell embraced the Malay with some affection. It appeared he was a regular visitor, and at dinner he regaled us with information about the island. Mr Tin described it as 'a Paradise on earth', as indeed it proved – although, as Bissell graphically explained, it had not been Paradise for some: skeletons minus the heads had recently been found in a cave, reputedly those of a party who had escaped in a naval motor-boat from the mainland following the swift Japanese advance in January 1942. Bombed by Zeros, they had run aground, and when the Japanese captured them they were beheaded.

Proper roads were few on the island – only rough paths led up into the rain forests. Fishermen, said to be Siamese, supplied the rest house. Marble was being extracted from a quarry at a place called Kisap, and I think it was near here that Mr Bissell showed us the Lake of the legendary White Crocodile, said to emerge periodically from the waters, which were very deep. I suppose it snatched small children.

Everything was going smoothly. The rest house cost only a few Straits dollars a night, thanks to the Sultan. The junk was scheduled to pick us up the morning of the fourth day, and return to Alor Star by late afternoon, giving me a few hours to motor-cycle back to Sungei Patani. I determined to enjoy my Paradise, and I did . . . until the day Mr Tin commented at break-fast that the junk was, exceptionally, returning on the fifth rather than the fourth day. I felt a cold shiver, and made mental com-putations. It should just work out: I had no parade on my fifth morning, and could arrive back pretending I had been testing the water at Gunong Jerai, an extinct volcano on the Merbok River which was the responsibility of my Hygiene Section. But I did not take the kindly Harbour Master into account. Solicitous for Captain Harris's well being, anxious that he should not be inconvenienced by the change of schedule, he telephoned to reassure the captain's superiors. Consternation! There was of course no record of 'Captain Harris, RAMC'. The Harbour Master was asked to examine the BSA, and it was identified as belonging to my RAMC Casualty Clearing Station. Military police were summoned, and they prepared to throw the book at me. In blissful ignorance of this hullabaloo I walked deserted beaches collecting a sackful of huge exotic shells.

As the junk tied up at Alor Star, my throat constricted: there stood two stiff-looking redcaps. I was arrested. 'But my motor-bike!' I protested. 'Already collected,' the redcaps replied. I was forced to leave my lovely shells on the junk. The redcaps had railway warrants for the night sleeper to Kuala Lumpur: I was being taken to HQ RAMC, not back to Sungei Patani. At least they were friendly, and I was not handcuffed like a felon. After an eight-hour journey I was taken straight in to my old acquaintance Colonel D'Arcy, marched into his presence by a severe-looking sergeant-major. The door closed.

Colonel D'Arcy smiled. 'Sit down, Harris,' he said. 'You've got yourself in a right mess.' Then he suddenly changed the subject. 'Williams-Hunt sends his regards. Told me of your visit with him to the Grik caves in the Bentong Mountains. Bit dangerous, I must say. He said your interest in Malayan archaeology was rare.' It was a shaft of sunlight, and I was relieved to be told that I could escape a court martial by agreeing to a Board of Enquiry chaired by him, and accepting its punishment. 'You'll probably lose a stripe,' he said. 'But we've taken into account your good record at Sungei Patani.'

The Board it was, the penalty as predicted. I left with D'Arcy's words ringing in my ears: 'You'll get murdered. Archaeology and the Emergency are not good bedfellows.' I met Williams-Hunt once more, for a second excursion to the caves, where he had been busily cutting through a thousand years of bat guano. The flint implements we found there were given to the museum in Taiping.

We were not murdered. In November 1951, my National Service at an end, I sailed for Europe and home, went pike-spinning on Slapton Lea in Devon with Uncle Sid, and then found myself in Paris.

10

Richard Penard, or 'La Transition est le style parfait'

Paris Calls

IT WAS OF course the proceeds of the kerosene fiddle that enabled me to go to Paris. I had been there before, in 1948, just for a week: arriving at the Gare du Nord, I made for the Sorbonne and the Left Bank, and found a tiny hotel in a narrow alleyway off the boulevard St-Germain. It struck me as conveniently quiet, huddled in by buildings, yet so near the clamorous boulevard. All night long the stairs creaked to footsteps ascending and footsteps descending. It was a brothel. I made my obeisance at its altar.

My choice of Paris after demobilisation on 9 December 1951 was influenced by a pile of tattered *Connoisseur* magazines in the Sergeant's Mess at Sungei Patani, dating from 1937 to August 1941. I often speculated upon their provenance. Did they originate with RAF Sungei Patani, or were they a memento of a local rubber planter, cut off from his subscription by the developing war? For me they were fine browsing fodder, and as no one else was remotely interested in them, they were relocated to my Hygiene office. In those days furniture and antiques were a monthly feature, and so the decorative arts germ was planted.

If it was decade-old magazines that introduced me to the decorative arts, it was Father Brandreth's Presbytery at St George's Anglo-Catholic church that introduced me to God. I found my way there through the intervention of a neighbour of my parents in Cowley, whose son worked in Paris and was an acolyte at St George's. Henry Renaud Turner Brandreth was an authority on Satanism with a fund of wicked but unauthenticated tales about Aleister Crowley, and claimed to have written the standard article on Satanism for the *Encyclopaedia Britannica*. I wish I had listened more carefully to his account of the satanism of Eric Satie and Émile Zola. The Presbytery was a watering-place for many literary-inclined Anglo-Catholics passing through Paris. In clouds of incense I was confirmed there on 11 January 1953 by the Bishop of Nyasaland, with Father Robert Pierce Casey, Chaplain of Sidney Sussex College, Cambridge in attendance. At my first confession the Bishop reeked of alcohol, and that evening Father Casey attempted my seduction. Ever since I have abstained from these pagan practices.

A Dutch philosophy student in London had revealed to me a ploy for survival in Paris: enrol at the École du Louvre, and thus acquire student status for lodgings, medical attention and use of the students' restaurants (or, rather, soup kitchens). I will say only that the French dental practice I experienced was little short of root murder, and as for lodgings, I was memorably housed at 1 rue des Cendriers, off the boulevard de Ménilmontent and, appropriately, near the Cimetière Père Lachaise.

I held out my student's *carte d'identité* as the door opened. The concierge wore an indescribably greasy red linen smock and a black woollen cap. I handed her my authorization papers, and mumbled something in my atrocious French about being '*heureux*' to be there, little knowing that my happiness would not last long. She led me to the front room, once the concierge's domain but now with its window giving on to the entrance passage papered over. I surveyed a simple scene that was a timeless encapsulation of artistic poverty: a coke stove in one corner, one bucket of coke, one shovel, a ramshackle iron bed with a disagreeable-looking mattress, two sheets and two blankets, one table and one chair, no cupboards, just hooks on the wall and a large flat shelf on which to place clothes. A small dirty triangular sink in one corner boasted a cold tap only. The general décor was as dirty and shabby as the concierge herself. No matter: this was the romantic Paris of poets, philosophers and artists.

Disillusion had set in even before my discovery that the sheets were never changed, and that every morning at 4.30 a noisome street stall set up outside the window. The toilet in the court-yard was pointed out but how foolish I was not to examine it before night fell. The courtyard was slippery underfoot. I opened a wooden door and could barely make out a hole of the squat sort, out of which emerged a suffocatingly disagreeable smell. There was no paper of course, so I retreated, returned, squatted, squeezed and papered. Then I rose and pulled the chain. There was no cleansing, sucking-away 'whoosh', just a sudden swirl of obnoxious floating foetid things around my shoes. Even now I cannot call to mind anything else, ever, quite as awful as having to wash my shoes in the cold water in my sink. For the next few weeks I peed in that sink, made regular use of the nearest public toilet (in the Père Lachaise cemetery), and became an habitué of a Napoleon II public baths somewhere near the Jardin des Plantes, a meeting-place of the high and low in Parisian society.

I had been bold enough to write to the Director of the Wallace Collection for advice about what I might usefully do in Paris, and received an unexpectedly warm reply from his deputy,

8. Sir Francis Watson, photographed in 1994

Francis Watson: 'See Richard Penard in my name. He's a collector of the greatest taste, and an old friend. I'll ring him.' I was told to meet Penard in a bistro on the avenue Marceau at seven. I would easily recognize him. And there he was: Richard Penard y Fernandez, a frail-looking gentleman with pale delicate face, white hands with bright blue veins, dressed in a light beige suit, darker beige shirt and blue tie. His shoes were brown and obviously by Lobb, his clothes expensive. He was the epitome of understated elegance. I sat down and we chatted. I was not invited to eat, but as we talked he picked away at a plate of sliced meats and sipped a glass of wine. Seemingly as an afterthought he offered me a glass of wine, which I accepted. But that was all.

Penard seemed very anglophile, and talked reflectively about London before the First World War, when he had contemplated living there. There was no trace of accent in his English. I guessed he was at least seventy, so he must have been born around 1880. He had been a member of the Argentinian diplomatic corps before the First World War, in Vienna, Berlin, Brussels, and London. He mentioned a nephew in Rio de Janeiro. 'You know Francis well?' he asked. I had to confess we had never met, but told him of the encouraging letters from London advising me on my putative career in furniture and the decorative arts. 'Francis is a wonderful man. Monsieur Verlet at Versailles speaks so highly of him. You must see my collection,' Richard continued, taking out his diary. I was to arrive at eleven o'clock in two days' time – not morning, but evening. 'I'm nocturnal,' he added with a smile. 'Now, goodbye,' and I was dismissed. I found him slightly brusque, but I think he was putting me to the test.

The address he gave me proved to be a nineteenth-century apartment block on rue Cognac Jay off the Quai d'Orsay. Just one bell, and unexpectedly it was Richard himself who answered, opening the door onto a hall with a flight of stairs focused upon a large landing. The facing wall was lined with books, all as I discovered later in precious bindings of royal provenance. As we reached this landing I noticed a recess on one side containing a truckle bed. Richard saw me eyeing it in surprise. 'I sleep here,' he said. I did wonder about the bathroom. We ascended to the main floor, and in passing through the door I entered a wonderland of the epoch of Louis XV and Louis XVI which has been described by others as a 'Grotto of Marvels'. 'I believe the Transitional Period between 1760 and 1770 to have been the perfection of French eighteenth-century art. I have always striven to collect in this style,' Richard stated.

Having recently studied the archives of the Paris firm of Carlhian et Cie, suppliers of panelling and decorators in conservative but exquisite taste, I now suspect Richard's suite of rooms to have been panelled and fitted out by Carlhian in the late 1920s. To my juvenile eye, however, they might have been Madame de Pompadour's own apartments in her château of Bellevue – and indeed, I later learned that the boiseries in what Richard called his white and gold boudoir came from Bellevue. In his *chambre à coucher*, where he never slept, the boiseries were by Rousseau. Today the decidedly twentieth-century ambience and Penard's contribution to it are clear to me. But what mattered then was his astonishing collection of works of art: furniture, paintings, bronzes, terracottas, porcelain, silver, carpets, fabrics, books, clocks and ornaments, all in his estimation a reflection of that Transitional style of the period when Louis Quinze passed into Louis Seize. To me, as to Penard, they seemed perfection, and so I joined him in his reverence.

Richard was a quiet but determined enthusiast. The detailed tour, object by object, was always *de rigueur*. There could have been no better education for a callow youth, and it was certainly

9. Richard Penard's Grand Salon in Paris

an improvement on the boring lectures at the École du Louvre. He never stinted the time that passed so quickly. In the antechamber was a coffer of wood, and in it was the one object I really lusted after: a perfect model of a little theatre painted by Louis-Carrosis Carmontelle on parchment and silk. Richard placed it in front of a lamp and turned a handle, and there scrolled past a series of transparencies specially painted for the duc d'Orléans: Rousseau's tomb at Ermenonville, the grotto at Méréville, a fête at the park of Moulin Joly, a park in the English style, and other scenes in the environs of Paris. In the *grand salon* were boiseries said to have come from the hôtel des Soeurs Haudriette on the rue Saint-Honoré and to have been carved by Jules Degoullons. Here and in all the rooms, so many objects and pieces of furniture had royal provenance: furniture by Roentgen, 'BVRB', Demay, Carlin, Jacob, many bronzes by Caffieri or Gouthière.

The *petit salon*, again with boiseries by Degoullons, was presided over by Bernini's bust of Cardinal Richelieu. Here, later, we had supper. The armchairs were by Cresson. A set of four pictures of the Seasons, ordered by Madame Geoffrin from Joseph Vien, were of amazing precocity. Richard obviously loved them. He stood in front of them and turned to me. 'Now, when do you think these were painted?' I guessed post-Revolution. 'No,' replied Richard with a smile. 'In 1769.' And so I passed through his rooms, item by item, transfixed: Madame de Sevigné by Mignard, Falconet's sculpture of Pygmalion, and so on and so on, until we came to the circular *petit boudoir*. This rotonda came from an *hôtel* on the chaussée d'Antin designed by or for the architect Belanger, and years later I recognized it among the Carlhian photographs conserved in the Getty Museum, confirmation of my guess that Calhian's firm did fit out Penard's rooms. It was a sort of titillation room. Here was

Richard's collection of naughty pictures, presided over by a draped terracotta nymph by Clodion. The drapery lifted off, to reveal pudenda with real hair. Richard claimed it was Madame de Pompadour's pubic hair, given to the sculptor by the marquise herself.

I was surprised to discover that it was half-past two in the morning. Richard was still fresh but I was groggy, besotted though I was with his collection, such a rare assemblage, presented with the very best of French *gout*. Suddenly, with that same veneer of brusqueness, my host said, 'That's enough! Time for a drink, and something to eat.' He left the room and returned pushing a trolley (never in the course of the eight nocturnal visits I made to Richard's *appartement* did I encounter a maid or manservant). To this day I cannot recall ever seeing another such trolley. It carried chilled champagne of renowned early vintage, and a remarkable selection of the finest pastries Paris could offer. I tentatively took one, and ate it slowly. With delight I watched as Richard scoffed not one, not two or three, but four or five. Many years later I thought of him as I watched a table of four German *frauleins* in the Orangery at Schloss Ansbach demolishing a *surtout de table* composed of similar pastries. The nocturnal Richard lived on pastries and champagne. At four o'clock sharp, just as if a stage curtain had come down, he sent me away, with a command to return at a later date. So in the dawn I crossed the pont de l'Alma to the Métro Alma Marceau, stopped off somewhere for coffee and a croissant, and returned to my grotty bed.

Always when I went to see Richard there was the same gourmet fare, for the eyes and for the stomach. He would require me to relate my daily discoveries in Paris and its environs. What did I think of this *hôtel* and that *hôtel*? How did I get access to the Désert de Retz? Did I not think the mass lectures at the École du Louvre quite the wrong way to learn about art? What had I found in the library of the Musée des Arts Décoratifs? (I had found an album of architectural designs by Bernardo Vittone.)

Some years after I had left Paris, Richard rose from his truckle bed one night, tripped on his dressing-gown cord, and fell down the stairs. There was no will, and his nephew put everything up for auction at the Palais Galliera on 7 December 1960. The Louvre pre-empted many lots. Bunny Mellon bought the Carmontelle theatre, and with Francis's advice Charlie and Jayne Wrightsman, billionaire benefactors of the Metropolitan Museum of Art, bought the best of what remained.

Privé – Défense d'entrer

The Désert de Retz

I FOUND THE teaching methods of the École du Louvre dispir-
iting. Professors declaimed lectures from a rostrum to a large
audience. There was no dialogue. So I ceased to attend. It was
six months before the authorities realized I was occupying
student accommodation (or, rather, a student slum), and enjoying student medical attention, but had disappeared from the halls
of the École. I had hit upon an alternative means of acquiring
an education in architecture and the decorative arts (I believe
may still be available). I refer to those groups who meet a guide,
usually outside a designated Métro station, with whom to
explore an area of Paris in detail for a fee of a few francs. One
afternoon it might be 'Les hôtels du Marais' or 'Les hôtels du rue
de Varennes', another 'La Sainte Chapelle', or 'La Chambre des
Députés', or an examination of 'Les ameublements de Louis
Seize au Musée des Arts Décoratifs'. Most of my companions on
these perambulations of artistic discovery were more or less
genteel, I suppose the equivalent of our present-day NADFAS
ladies, but one or two were decidedly aristocratic: a duchesse
here, a comtesse there. At first they regarded askance the young

Englishman with his fumbling, atrocious French, but later, when I had been a regular for a few months, I was accepted, and even invited to what they called the *après-thé*, which meant cream cakes!

We also made excursions in the environs of Paris. Several were to examine what survived of wholly or partially demolished royal châteaux: Sceaux, Saint-Cloud, Louveciennes. One afternoon we walked the ghostly outlines of the lost gardens and layout of Louis XIV's Marly le Roi, whose ruined château and pavilions had been finally demolished in 1816. On the way there our coach followed green roads through the degraded forest of Marly (this was long before the beastly A13 *autoroute* cut its devastating swathe of environmental pollution through it).

We were driving along a ride somewhere near the small village of Retz when our guide, Madame Piçon, pointed out the Ferme de Retz by the roadside. 'We're near M. Racine de Monville's famous Désert de Retz,' she said – I knew of this eighteenth-century ornamental garden by reputation – adding a little bitterly that the owner, Monsieur Albert Passy, was '*très difficile*', as well as '*agressif*', and always refused her pleas to visit. During our drive back to Paris Madame Piçon told us all about the scandal of the Désert, how there appeared to be no way of compelling the owner to maintain the garden's historic monuments. It was all too tantalizing: I was determined to see the Désert, denied to so many.

At the library of the Musée des Arts Décoratifs I was able to look at Georges-Louis Le Rouge's *Jardins anglo-chinois à la mode* in its thirteenth *cahier* of 1785. The engraved views whetted my appetite. I could scarcely believe that the Broken Column House and the Maison Chinoise might have survived. I decided *my* approach would be more circuitous and secret than Madame Piçon's: I would avoid the Ferme de Retz, and the '*agressif*' M.

Passy. Two buses took me to the village of St Nom on the edge of the Forêt de Marly. I walked a mile or so along a lane and then struck off into forest rides. I have a fair sense of direction, but it was serendipity that enabled me to find the Désert on my first cast, on the ride out of the forest leading to what is known as the Grotto Entrance. On a wayside tree was a large wooden sign: 'PRIVÉ – DÉFENSE D'ENTRER'. I noted with relief that it was very weather-worn.

At this juncture I must jump a little ahead in time to recall a conversation I had with Geoffrey Houghton Brown in 1954. He asked whether I had ever seen the Désert de Retz and I was able to reply, 'Why, yes,' and give him an account, as I give it now, of my experience. Geoffrey agreed that there was no other surviving 'exotic' garden like the Désert; indeed, as a collector of country houses and their appurtenances, he wanted to buy it. He had gone there with John Fowler and Ian McCallum in the spring of 1950, following the publication in November 1949 of an article by Osvald Sirén in the *Architectural Review*, where Ian was an editor. Sirén's article caused a sensation in London and few now remember how many English *aficionados* made for the Désert as a result of it – David Vicary, Jonathan Vickers, David Styles, Felix Harbord. It was essentially a foretaste of Sirén's *China and the Gardens of Europe of the Eighteenth Century* that came out the following year, a book I did not discover until 1959. I should also add that although the Désert had been the subject of much publicity in Paris when it was listed in 1941 as a *Monument Historique classé*, it went into limbo during the war years and after, unprotected from decay. Indeed, it was only in 1966, thanks to André Malraux's *Loi Malraux* 'Concerning Historic Monuments', a legislative means of saving such monuments, that it received an umbrella of protection – but by then the Maison Chinoise had gone. I have never been able to discover exactly when.

Mature reflection has led me to the view that M. de Monville's garden buildings and ornaments were overcrowded, that the Désert de Retz lacked the expansive layout and properly designed landscape setting of, for example, Painshill – also photographed by Sirén for his book – and that this was typical of many French 'Picturesque' gardens. At the time, however, the Désert seemed to many the *ne plus ultra* of an abandoned garden.

In its heyday the Grotto Entrance of the Désert must have been spectacular. Just two blocks survived of this vast rusticated, almost megalithic stone portal, taken from Piranesi's *Carceri*. The wooden door was still there, but the grotto behind it was only a pile of stones and tufa. It is difficult now to remember exactly what the Désert was like when I first saw it. Today M. de Monville's gardens is as well documented as any in France – although vigorous dispute still rages as to whether Hubert Robert contributed to its making. I contest this: the garden bears all the hallmarks of Racine de Monville as its amateur designer. As its present owner and saviour M. Choppin de Janvry has shown, however, de Monville did have an *exécutant* in François Barbier, a garden architect.

In 1952 all demarcations had been obliterated by brambles, and nearly all the buildings were covered with creepers and surface ivy. The first to catch my eye from the entrance, to my left, was the Pyramid (called by Le Rouge *La Glacière*), looking like nothing more than a pile of ivied stones. The apprehensive silence of trespass lay heavy upon me: I was distracted from the Ruined Gothic Church beyond by a glimpse of the Broken Column House through the tracery outline of a vast linden tree. I almost burst with glee. André Breton and his Surrealists were fascinated by this edifice, which functioned as a proper house, furnished in a simplified Louis Seize style; they saw the *bizarrerie* in it, as they did in the 'Palais Idéal' of the Postman Cheval at Hauterives, that strange temple to Nature in the Drôme.

The door to the Column House was broken down, the vestibule derelict. Fallen plaster, splintered wood battens, lumps of stonework, dusty bricks formed piles to be climbed over to get to the spiral stair, which at first glance appeared to defy ascent, not so much from its precarious condition as because of the rubbish blocking the way and the nursery of cats that scattered at my approach. Much of the upstairs décor had survived, however. The reception *salons* were on the third floor, for the view across the gardens through oval windows, and here, as Sirén had discovered, the pretty Louis Seize chimney-pieces were still intact. There were also the unpleasantnesses all too familiar to me from my explorations of empty English country houses: broken glass bottles, human excrement, paper rubbish – all the evidences of temporary and alien refuge. And then, framed by an oval window, I spied the roof of the Maison Chinoise. I shivered with anticipation and went scurrying down the stair, afraid I might be apprehended by the '*agressif*' farmer Passy before I had had a proper look at this most famous of all European Chinese houses.

Recent studies seem to have concluded the date of the Maison Chinoise to be the early 1780s, following the construction of the Broken Column House between 1781 and 1782, rather than the earlier date of 1778–9 traditionally assigned to it. Having lately written about the Dröttningholm China House, built in 1763, I am just now surfeited with European chinoiserie, but neither this nor half a century as an architectural historian can dim the memory of the profound emotion of my first encounter with a chinoiserie building. There it stood, in terrible and terminal

10. The Maison Chinoise, at the Désert de Retz in 1947

decay, yet somehow electrifying. Of course I was too ignorant to recognize it for what it was, a Western European interpretation of Chinese originals, the invention of the Physiocrat Racine de Monville; only later did I analyse it and compare it with the more authentic Chinese houses in Sir William Chambers's *Designs of Chinese Buildings* (1757).

Pushing upon a varnished door, I realized why Sirén had published no photographs of the interior. All was darkness: the window shutters had been nailed up. I don't know whether he ever ventured upstairs; I did. The door leading off the stairs opened with a hefty push to reveal a well-lit room panelled in acajou wood, recognizably a library. A photograph taken about 1900 survives, clearly showing the skilful and graceful harmonization of Chinese and Louis Seize elements. A pantry still retained its beautiful beaten-copper sink, and in the ground-floor bedroom there were scraps of an orange-patterned silk on the walls. But something I saw, and Sirén did not, was particularly exciting: half a dozen or more rectangular panels stacked against the wall, painted and varnished with green and brownish chinoiserie subjects. No doubt when the Maison Chinoise vanished they disappeared into the maw of an *antiquaire*.

Then came the heart-stopping moment. Still in the upper *salon*, I heard crunching footsteps and barking dogs. I furtively peered from a window, to see an elderly, rough-looking man with a gun under his arm, accompanied by two largish dogs with pointed snouts, running about in circles, sniffing excitedly. They went into the Broken Column House, came out, then circled it. As they approached the Maison Chinoise I withdrew into the far corner of the room, petrified by the thought of canine assault, ill-wrought excuses in bad French whizzing through my mind. I heard noises from below, then a step on the stair . . . but no more. Amazingly, it seemed they were *not* following my scent. A command to the dogs rang out, crunching footsteps faded away, silence descended. I must wait, I knew, so I curled up in a corner, and until dusk approached amused myself with day-dreams in which I took down de Monville's books from the shelves, imagined him discussing with M. Barbier his design for the Chinese House. He lived in the Broken Column House, I thought, and used the ground-floor bedroom of the Maison Chinoise for amorous pleasures. It all seemed right and proper.

When I thought it was safe to leave I paused downstairs to cast a covetous glance at the painted panels, then left the way I had come. I have been unable to this day to reconstruct my return to the rue des Cendriers near Père Lachaise. It certainly involved a long walk with no hitch-hikes, and no buses until Porte d'Auteil.

I returned to the Désert in the 1980s with Monique Mosser and Phyllis Lambert, as guests of Choppin de Janvry. He could never believe I had been there so long before him – nor I think did he believe the fervour with which we of perfidious Albion had taken the Désert to our hearts in the late 1940s. His saving of the Désert is an epic in the history of garden conservation, of course. But I will permit myself the same naughty note of dissent I expressed about Painshill in *No Voice from the Hall*: like Painshill, the Désert has, to my mind, been saved at the expense of the romance of decay and ruin. André Breton would not like it today – but then, we can't have our cake and eat it, can we?

12

Out of reach of feisty knights

RECENTLY, IN A box of old French postcards, I found a grimy envelope. In it was my admission card to the École du Louvre for 1952. Also in that envelope was a roughly scribbled sketch of a curious wooden object, wherein lies a tale.

Fifty years ago the Marais and the 1st *arrondissement* had not been gentrified. Around the Musée Carnavelet historic *hôtels* remained, now in commercial use: the lovely domestic architecture of the Parisian town-house was falling into disuse and decay. Parts of the Marais had not changed since the photographer Eugène Atget saw them through his lenses in the early years of the century. One day, walking along a narrow street, I was brought up short by a *coup d'oeil* through a late seventeenth-century portal and into a courtyard. The cobblestones sprouted grass. In a corner lay a pile of broken fragments of ornamental stonework which looked medieval, perhaps from a church restoration. To one side were propped planks of carved wooden panelling, bleached and rotted by exposure to the sun and the other elements. Opposite, against a row of windows, stood a bulky eighteenth-century black leather coach, ruined beyond redemption, weeds growing up around the wheels. One door was off, and it had become a cattery. The arched portal was obviously the proscenium for the stage of an *antiquaire*.

Sensitive about the deficiencies of my French, I poked my head surreptitiously and quietly into the hall that opened off the courtyard. It was crammed with the detritus of possession: a tumbled medley of chairs, mostly painted, and bereft of upholstery; a pair of gilt pier glasses, the glass of one shattered; what appeared to be a very fine rococo stone urn. Dust lay thick over all. The antique dealers of today tend to be squeaky clean, their goods tidily set out, dusted and polished, but I suspect my *antiquaire* and his predecessors had been commonplace in Paris ever since dealers set themselves up to take advantage of the disposals which followed the Revolution.

Out of a side room shuffled the *antiquaire* himself, elderly and dishevelled. I can see him now, for his goatee beard resembled my son Lucian's. I would not have noticed his black-and-grey-striped evening-dress trousers, had it not been for the sandals he wore, from which his yellowing toe-nails protruded (always an attractive sight, and one I've all too recently encountered at an architectural drawings conference in Oxford). '*Je suis interessé en l'ameublement historique,*' I muttered in my impeccable French. He gestured me in and waved a hand in the direction of further rooms.

Of course, I was not yet working as a lowly assistant in the antique shop belonging to Geoffrey Houghton Brown and Francis Collin. Had I possessed more than my kerosene legacy, I might have made a killing. My *antiquaire* had four superb rococo ormolu wall lights, not quite as fine as the elaborate rococo of Meissonnier, but pretty near his style. He was asking about a hundred and twenty pounds for the set. I was also attracted to a fragment from an eighteenth-century organ loft, a five-foot-high console with two putti blowing trumpets. What struck me particularly was the musty smell of objects in place for decades, acquiring immutability. Several years later, staying at Hector Binney's Wulf Hall in 1955 (as recounted in *No Voice from the Hall*), I was vividly reminded of that ambience, and that *antiquaire*. I had indeed already spoken to Geoffrey about the shop, but he was not encouraged to go there, for at this date it was nothing exceptional, and here in England there were hundreds of antique shops crammed with desirable things. It was, after all, the time of our own disposals from the homes of the landed classes.

But this tale is about one object that caught my attention that day. So puzzling was it that I made the sketch disinterred from the postcard box. It was a massive cube of wood, very crudely shaped, as if hacked with an axe, about two feet square, with a length of coarse, rusted iron chain firmly fixed into one side. The chain had obviously once been longer, for it appeared to have been sawn off comparatively recently. On the other five faces of the cube were pairs of iron hooks set about three inches apart. I stared at it. What was it? My first guess, that it came from a country-house game larder, I dismissed because of the weight of the block. Yet the chain suggested that it must have hung from something, somewhere. The *antiquaire* shuffled in. '*Mon Dieu, c'est très mystérieuse,*' I said, to which he replied simply '*D'accord*' – and then, shaking his head, he went on: '*Il est très vieux. J'ai l'achetée de la Château de Beaurepaire après La Grande Guerre.*' So it had been lying there for more than thirty years.

Time passed, time that spanned my days at the Fulham Road antique shop and my early years at the RIBA. It might have been 1964, and Eileen and I were at the Grosvenor House Antiques

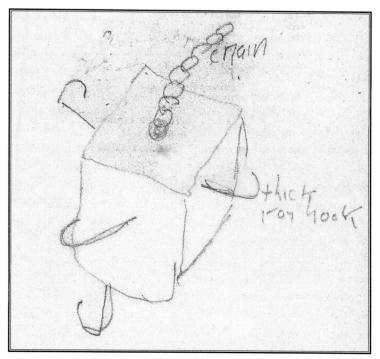

11. Drawing of the mysterious Block seen in Paris, 1952

Fair. I halted suddenly in front of Ronald E. Lee's stand – or, since my memory sometimes serves me ill, maybe it was Wolsey's – and gave a shout. There, illumined by a spot-light, was THE BLOCK! But no – it was another, for it lacked the chain. Ronnie (if it was indeed he) explained that feisty medieval knights were known to be always spoiling for a fight, so that when they visited a castle they were required to hand in their swords for safe-keeping – to be hung from the hooks in a block such as this and hauled up to the ceiling well out of reach. Ronnie was con-vinced his block was unique, and not at all inclined to believe my tale, but when I returned that afternoon to show him my sketch he was both shaken and incredulous. He pressed me to go back to Paris to see whether the shop still existed. Naughtily, I allowed him to pay my fare and hotel costs for two nights. Through my acquaintance with the de Magny family, who had lived in the Marais for many years, I was able to discover that my *antiquaire* was no more. He had died around 1954 and his shop had been, they said regretfully, '*écuré*', meaning 'cleaned out'. I can see my block being carted away in a tumbril – in more modern parlance, a skip. I like to think of it in use, as it once was, hanging in the Château of Amboise, perhaps, and bristling with the swords of feisty knights carousing in the Great Banqueting Hall below.

13

Happy takings

Battersea Pleasure Gardens

WHEN MY KEROSENE legacy ran out, I had regretfully to bring my stay in Paris to an end. I was now a vagrant in London, with only a few sixpences in my pocket and no job: a crisis loomed. But the bush telegraph in Bunje's Coffee House in Litchfield Street signalled that there was casual work to be found at Battersea Pleasure Gardens and Fun Fair. It was said that everyone was on the make, no questions were asked, and employees came and went like water through a colander. But first I had to find somewhere to live. Behind Lindsay House on the Chelsea Embankment lay that most secret of all London's gardens, the Moravian Burial Ground, and against its high and ancient brick walls on Milman's Street was a Salvation Army hostel. The wooden cubicle alloted me by the warden absorbed my last sixpence.

Because I was doing my National Service in Malaya during most of that year, the Festival of Britain in 1951 had passed me by, and I remained completely uninformed about its architectural significance. However, for one shilling and sixpence it was still possible to buy the *Guide* to the Pleasure Gardens, with its

12. Cover of the Battersea Pleasure Gardens *Guide*, 1951

moderne cover by Hans Tisdall. Recently I found this booklet in my library, and was greatly struck by the list of artists and designers involved. What a contrast with the banality of the Millennium Dome. The Pleasure Gardens were pure joy: 'We aim at Beauty and pursue the Gay' wrote A.P. Herbert in his poem extolling them. Osbert Lancaster designed the Entrance and Fountains of the Grand Vista, John Piper the Grand Vista itself – as well as Tea Houses, Rotundas, Lakes and Fern Houses – Lawrence Scarfe the Punch and Judy Show and Magic Shop, Russell Page all the landscaping and gardens, Rowland Emmett the delightful Far Tottering and Oyster Creek Railway, Hugh Casson the Aviary Restaurant, and Guy Sheppard the Riverside Theatre and Schweppes's Grotto. It was this last that was to prove my undoing.

To get into the gardens you paid the admission charge and passed through a turnstile. It would be my job to man an entry-point and take the money, as spelled out for me by Tommy Edge, the shifty manager. 'We watch you all the time,' he warned, 'and if you're caught passing visitors outside the turnstiles it's the sack, and you're docked half your first weekly wage.' Fire regulations required a emergency passage of open access at each turnstile, so there was always a temptation, especially with large groups of schoolchildren, to take, say, twenty sixpences and pass most of the party through the fire access. If this were to be done ten times a day – well, two hundred sixpences added up to five pounds, and in 1953 this was more than an average weekly wage.

I discovered that I had joined a confraternity of petty criminals. Almost every operation was carried on to the benefit of the employees rather than the London County Council. Sleaze – though we didn't call it that then – was rampant. Behind the pasteboard façades of stalls were nests of drug dealers, pickpockets and busy prostitutes in caravans. An attractive girl charged

two pounds a trick. It was all in the best Vauxhall Gardens tradition, of course.

Initially I behaved so well that after two weeks Tommy Edge
promoted me from the west entrance gates, near the administra-
tion block, to Guy Sheppard's Schweppes's Grotto of the Four
Elements. I loved this enchanted underworld of technicolour
caverns and fragrant scents. In the Temple of the Winds four
breezes blew – the East Wind, for example, carried the smell of
spices and the sound of temple bells. In the Cave of Fire a bridge
crossed a volcanic pit hissing and bubbling with molten lava.
Earth was a cave with minerals and stalactites, where a glimmer-
ing pale phosphorescent blue fountain rose and fell, and Water
was a grotto-world of fish, strange sea creatures and sub-oceanic
corals. It was a popular venue for children, and surveillance of
the entrance was difficult: now the temptress sang her siren song.
On a weekend, five hundred or more might pass through each
day. After six weeks in the fairy's cavern I had creamed off at least
six months' salary. I had joined the confraternity!

The ease of making these petty gains led me to speculate
about managerial amnesia in recording the attendance figures.
The turnstiles clocked up the visitors, but I could never understand why, after each thousand, Tommy or one of his myrmi-
dons would re-set the clock to zero. At the end of each day an
assistant made the rounds of the turnstiles to record the figures,
followed by two security men who would empty the cash boxes.
Then all was made clear. One evening the assistant asked me for
a light, and put down his record book to take the matches. As he
lit up I saw he had noted 650 in the book, not the 900 on the
clock. Now I realized why the clock was turned back at each
thousand. Once returned to zero, the record was lost. It was a
scam. Having made this discovery, I threw caution to the winds,
and passed as many as possible through the fire access. Of course,

it soon became obvious from the management's records that the Grotto of the Four Elements had somehow lost its fascination. I was summoned and dismissed, but the smirk on Tommy's face was wiped away when I casually remarked that I had kept a record of his every misreading of the clock. As I left the room, I shouted, 'Happy takings!'

14

A drifters' paradise

Corsham Court

I N THE LATE autumn of 1952 a postcard arrived for me from Eric Degg, student potter under James Tower at the Bath Academy of Art, housed in Lord Methuen's Corsham Court since 1946. It was a liberal and fertile art school, combining tuition in painting, sculpture, pottery and fabric design with literature, poetry and music. 'Come and stay for as long as you like,' Eric implored me. I had met him early in 1950 on National Service in the Royal Army Medical Corps, but had come to know of Corsham more recently because Lord Methuen, the painter-peer, was a friend of Francis Watson. Eric had been badgering me to go down to see him since my return from Paris. Corsham was not difficult to hitch-hike to, and I found Eric in Beechfield, an attractive late-Georgian bow-fronted house in the village of Pickwick, just north of Corsham. I remember some rooms and the staircase painted with modern murals, which I only later discovered were the work of Peter Potworowski, who was one of the tutors, and his pupils. I later came to know Pickwick well because of Robin Eden's glorious antique shop there, regularly plundered by

13. Beechfield, Pickwick, Corsham, Wiltshire, 1960s, showing the Pottery Studio (Keith Farr)

Geoffrey Houghton Brown for his shops on the Fulham Road and in Buckinghamshire.

Eric pointed to a mattress on the floor of his room, where I was to sleep, and explained the set-up. Beechfield was the men's lodging, and the women were housed in Monks Park, south of Corsham (the intention was that the twain should meet only for meals and instruction at the Court; but, as I was soon to discover, the twain met very frequently indeed, and in more conducive circumstances). The arrangements at Corsham might have been specifically designed to be taken advantage of by anyone of itin-erant inclinations. Eric pointed out two men and three women who had been living at the Court 'illegally' for several months. No one was scrutinized when queuing for grub, so they would take their meals in the dining hall in the Court and then disap-pear into the woods and fields. It may only be hearsay, but one William Marriner is reputed to have spent the years 1951 and 1952 drifting in and out whenever he needed consolation from his girl friend, a sculptress studying under Kenneth Armitage.

For two weeks I joined the meals queue, morning and evening. As Degg had written on his postcard, 'It's a drifter's paradise.' Many years later in Japan I met James Kirkup, who had been the resident poet at Corsham. He acknowledged the laxity of the organization, but felt that it went with the liberalism of the tuition and matched a certain unfettered quality peculiar to the Corsham students.

Kirkup's use of the word 'unfettered' stirred recollections of the promiscuity of those students who were so inclined. Eric had remarked, apropos the curvaceous attractions of Roz Frink, that they matched her abilities as a painter. She was reputed to be the 'star of the show' at Corsham, the best student of Peter Pot (as he was known), who raved about her. Eric thought I'd take to her, although she had a reputation for being aloof. She was indeed attractive, in a busty way. I failed to bed her, but in her company enjoyed an incident I still remember with pleasure.

Roz and I hit the hitch-hiker's road with the intention of finding the lost demesne of Ashley Coombe, a Plinian Roman villa designed in the 1830s by Lady Lovelace on a seaside headland near Porlock in North Somerset which could only be approached by a hundred-yard-long tunnel through the cliffs. We took a slight detour to call at her parents' home, a cottage on the Fox-Pitt estate at Bishop's Caundle in Dorset. Her father was a cowman, and the contrast between the simple, earthy parents and their worldly and artistic daughter was somehow jarring. I sensed unhappy cross-currents, and was more than ready to move on the next morning.

We were now westward-bound, and just beyond Yeovil we flagged down a car driven by a handsome young businessman on his way to Barnstaple. When as was my rude habit I made for the front seat, Roz told me sharply to sit in the back, where I became the unwilling witness of an infuriating petting session conducted by means of eye contact and verbal innuendo. I flushed with irritation when he gave her his card and received her promise to communicate, and vowed to avenge this humiliation.

When we stopped at The Star at Watchet, I might not have existed. I was ignored when they ordered from the bar menu, at the table they were preoccupied with kneesie and footsie – they might just as well have been holding hands. I plotted my revenge. When their food had been served I took my drink over to their table, which annoyed them, and then excused myself. They did not so much as look up, no doubt hoping I might flush myself away down the pan. On my way past the buffet I grabbed a handful of lump sugar. In the car park I furtively let down all the tyres with the help of my biro, then unscrewed the petrol cap and popped the sugar in the tank (where in due course it would cause the engine to seize). With a final apprehensive glance at the pub I hit the road, taking the 'low' rather than the 'high', just in case they somehow managed to give chase. Once back at Beechfield I told Eric what had happened, ending with, 'Got to bugger off before Roz returns'. He found the tale of Harris's Revenge hilarious.

I met Roz once again a few years later, in odd circumstances. In 1959 at Alwyne Villas in Canonbury, where I lived for a while with Jack Woods-Palmer, an elderly couple who were guests at dinner said, 'Believe you used to know Roz Frink at Corsham. We look after her,' without explaining what 'look after her' meant. I related the Watchet incident and remarked casually that I wouldn't mind meeting her again. They seemed wary. 'She's changed a lot,' they said, but subsequently arranged for us to meet in The Salisbury, a pub in St Martin's Lane which in those days was a notorious gay watering-hole. She paused in the doorway, looking very different from the girl I had known. I guess she never fulfilled Peter Pot's expectations. He disappeared into Communist Poland, expecting to be treated as the Grand Old Man of Polish painting – but he was not, could not return, and died in despair. When I eventually returned to Ashley Coombe, I made a point of stopping at The Star in Watchet. The ruffian returned to the scene of his crime, and savoured it anew.

15

The way to Thurloe Square

I F FRANCIS WATSON was the first person I wrote to in the art world, he was also the first I met upon my return to London from Paris, late in 1953. It was with some apprehension that I rang him at the Wallace Collection, where he was still Deputy Director, but in the most friendly way he said, 'Come to dinner – why not tonight? At 8 Groom Place.' Here I met his wife Jane, and the cats. I think there were eleven in permanent residence at that time. Some years later, after our marriage, I took Eileen there, and when she offered to help Jane in the kitchen she was surprised to find, lined up on a shelf, half a dozen saucepans, all occupied by cats. At Jane's death in 1969 the total number of cats under her care, boarded out or in residence, was eighty-three. She found stray cats, took them in, and then placed advertisements in *The Lady*: 'Elderly and genteel clergyman must retire to nursing home. Will a kindly soul look after his ginger tabby?'

Groom Place: Douglas Cooper, the art historian and collector, had given Francis the remaining years on the lease of Number 8 when he went to Paris in 1939 or 1940 to join an ambulance unit. Douglas has passed into legend as a profane monster in his relations with friends and lovers. Of all those who became physically or mentally embroiled with Douglas, Francis alone retained his affections to the end; but then, Francis did not compete with Douglas in the world of modern art, or pose any threat; unlike John Richardson, who has written so vividly about him in *The Sorcerer's Apprentice: Picasso, Provence and Douglas Cooper.* Francis's relationship with the tetchy Charles F. Bell, a celebrated Keeper of Fine Art at the Ashmolean Museum, was perhaps different. Their relationship was tempestuous, but it held throughout Francis's marriage, and forty years later Francis regularly visited the senile Bell in a grubby old people's home on the traffic canyon that is Redcliffe Gardens, as I know, for I once accompanied him there. I have Bell's annotated volumes of the Wren Society's publications. Bell's hatred of Sir Kenneth Clark was venomous, and we all await the release of Bell's annotated copies of Clark's books, consigned to the Bodleian for a period of detention because of his scabrous and vindictive comments. They are time-bombs waiting to explode.

In the early 1950s I still felt a strong pull towards furniture and the decorative arts, despite my growing interest in architecture. Francis mentioned me to Anthony Blunt, who had been asked by Nikolaus Pevsner to recommend someone to work in the editorial department at Penguin Books, assisting with the 'Buildings of England' series. I found myself in offices on the old A40 at Harmondsworth, near Heathrow, now engulfed by the airport. When Pevsner interviewed me, he told me flatly that I needed a degree to be an architectural historian, and suggested I study part-time at Birbeck College: I was not so inclined, and was able to prove him wrong. I have described elsewhere my differences with Nikolaus, and even in 1953 I was aware of the curious fact that he never referred to the country house crisis. As a youth-hosteller, vagrant and hitch-hiker, I was captivated by the many

empty country houses I came across on my wanderings.
Nikolaus was also travelling through England at this time and all
through those critical years up to 1974, and he must have seen
hundreds of empty houses, yet not once did he allude to them
in the introductions to his county volumes. In any case, I was
quite unsuited to editing, and loathed the atmosphere at Penguin
Books. But Nikolaus's too-Teutonic quip to his secretary when
I was in his office in Gower Street – 'Treat him like a servant' –
was what did for me. I knew I did not belong, and within the
probation period I had been told to clear my desk. Uncle Sid
consoled me with a visit to an auction sale, I think at Campsey
Ash in Suffolk, and Francis took me out to lunch.

Francis had spoken of me to two people, Peter Wilson at
Sotheby's and Geoffrey Houghton Brown, and in May or June
1954 I was invited to meet both. 'Yes, we'd like you here,' said
Peter at my interview. 'Start you with English furniture.' I had
been outspoken about the primacy of architectural history over
that of the decorative arts, but there was that little matter of the
degree that Pevsner had deemed so essential. Francis lauded the
advantages of the decorative arts in this respect – 'No doctors in
the Wallace Collection,' he delighted in saying. Peter offered me
the job, terms and salary to be confirmed. But Fate had other
ideas. That very afternoon I had been asked to have tea with
Geoffrey at 20 Thurloe Square, South Kensington. Miss Hall the
housekeeper met me at the door, and I went up to Geoffrey's
room on the first floor and into a world of rich wall coverings,
Axminster carpets, Boulle and painted furniture. He and his
partner Francis Collin needed an assistant in their newly-opened
shop, Collin and Winslow on the Fulham Road, and in addition
Geoffrey needed help at Winslow Hall in Buckinghamshire. I
could hardly pay attention, for I was gazing in wonder at the
sumptuous elegance surrounding me. Geoffrey asked me where

14. 20 Thurloe Square, London, SW7: Geoffrey Houghton Brown's Salon, 1958

I lived, and I shrugged dismissively: at the time I was in a room overlooking the Seven Dials. 'Come downstairs,' Geoffrey said. 'I have a room in the basement.' It was watched over by Alessandro Vittoria's *Doge Andrea Gritti*, the furniture was elegant, the ambience congenial, the rent twenty-five shillings a week – I had hardly glanced around the room before my mind was made up. Not so much the Judgement of Solomon as the Judgement of Harris. The next day brought a letter from Peter Wilson welcoming me to Sotheby's. Life would have been very different there.

I soon began to make new friends and discover new mentors. Geoffrey was one, Rupert Gunnis at Hungershall Lodge in Tunbridge Wells another. I began to correspond with Howard

Colvin in Oxford. It must have been about this time, too, that I began to see Francis Watson on a regular basis. As a teller of tales, I doubt if he had an equal. As Truman Capote was to John Richardson, to me he was 'in the great tradition of homosexual raconteurs', and enlivened any assembly. The timbre of his voice was what made him exceptional. It put me in mind of General Fitzwilliam's description of Horace Walpole's conversation: 'He talked like a shooting star, or like Uriel, gliding on a sunbeam.' Alas that no one recorded Francis. He telephoned us in Gloucestershire a month before his death in September 1992: 'I'm coming over to see you. Think of a place to visit.' He was dying of bowel cancer. We went to see the derelict church of St Arild at Oldbury-on-the-Hill, and the ancient Tortworth Chestnut, then after lunch he spent the whole afternoon reciting limericks. We ached with laughter.

Anecdotes of the marriage of Francis and Jane are legendary. John Richardson likened her to a monkey, and how right he was. And her family came from Gibraltar. When Francis and Jane married in 1941, the Australian painter Roy de Maistre commented, 'We were all disappointed.' Francis revelled in the denigration meted out to him by Jane. They jousted constantly. The first time I dined with them in Groom Place they both rocked with laughter over a recent incident. Francis had been bicycling along old Park Lane one morning, without a jacket, when first he was drenched by a sudden shower of rain, and then to his dismay his chain came off. On the grass verge he wrestled to get the black oily chain back onto its cogs, but without success. At ten o'clock he was due at the Wallace Collection to meet the Metropolitan Museum of Art patrons Charlie and Jayne Wrightsman. As he stood with the rain making runnels down his grease-smeared face, damning the bike, Providence apparently relented and a taxi drew up. Its window slid down to reveal

Jane's face, contorted with laughter. Francis turned with relief to dump the bike on the pavement, but as he did so there was a further burst of shrill hilarity from Jane, up shot the window, and she was driven off. The Director of the Wallace Collection — as he now was — arrived in Manchester Square looking like the Wrightsmans' garage mechanic.

Eileen's favourite story is of the time she was expecting Jane to dinner and Francis telephoned from Groom Place. Jane would be late: she had found a stray lamb on the Quantock hills (where they rented a cottage), and was bringing it back on the train in a dog-collar and lead. There was doubt as to whether a taxi could be persuaded to bring it from Waterloo, and whether it would get on with the cats.

16

'I believe it is the drains, sir'

I FREQUENTLY RETURN in memory to the hallowed precincts of 20 Thurloe Square. Even today, when I am on the way to the Victoria and Albert Museum, I sometimes make a diversion from the Brompton Road by way of Alexander Place to peer down into what was my basement. At each end of a long stone-flagged passage were identical rooms. The one facing the Square was Miss Hall the housekeeper's bedroom, and the other, facing the garden, was my room, with a kitchen extension and a door to the garden through which I enjoyed sole access. Our shared bathroom opened off the middle of the passage. When the house was first built, in the 1840s, it had been the sitting-room for the cook and maids, so it was too large for just a bath, even one with an attendant gas-fired geyser of antique vintage. This seemed likely to explode at any time, roaring and blustering with that now all-but-forgotten gaseous smell, spurting out hot water in intermittent gushes. One end of the room was piled to the ceiling with old steamer trunks and assorted suitcases in leather and canvas.

The furniture in my room was Geoffrey Houghton Brown's,

and he was able to reel off the provenance of all the principal items. A Regency bookcase against one wall had come from the Weald Hall sale in 1950. The other walls were covered with red damask from the saloon at Eywood in Herefordshire. The white marble chimney-piece was late Georgian, from Formosa Place in Berkshire. The Axminster carpet, bought from an antique shop in Olney in Buckinghamshire, had come from Soane's Sulby Hall in Northamptonshire. And, as I have said, all was dominated, perhaps even overshadowed, by Vittoria's bust of Doge Andrea Gritti.

One day there was a knock on my door, and Miss Hall popped her head in. 'There's a smell here,' she said. 'I believe it is the drains, sir. Have you smelt it?' I had, but I rose, poked my head into the passage, sniffed affirmatively, and tried to reassure her. 'It'll probably go away.' It did not. It grew worse, an awful stink of rotten cheese, or effluent. Miss Hall rang the health department of the Kensington council, and two men arrived the next day. They examined the toilet, peered under a sewer-cover in the basement area, made suitably disgusted noises, and spoke of 'a stoppage' or 'a leak'. They promised to return. The stink grew still worse. Ronald Fleming, Geoffrey's 'old stick' of a friend who lived on the ground floor, grumbled to Miss Hall to hasten the council men's return. True to their promise, back they came. The stench was now so heavy as to be almost unbearable. 'We're afraid it's a road job,' they said.

Two days later a hammering bedlam of drilling broke out in the road. Alexander Place was closed off where it came into Thurloe Square, a trench was dug across the street, and pipes were exposed. The neighbouring house on the corner, 18 Thurloe Square, suffered the indignity of having its basement area paving lifted up for more drains to be examined. A crack was found. Chatting to the diggers, I asked, 'But if it's here, why do we smell it over there, around our bathroom, and they don't smell it here?' This was clearly too difficult. 'Oh, it travels along the pipes,' they shrugged. During the day, up came a portion of pipe and a new section was introduced. The stench in our house did not diminish.

Because of the smell I had been giving my usual bath a miss – but the condition of my under-arms was by now beginning to rival the miasma, so I filled the tub and added fragrant unguents. As I lay there, peering out over the bubbles, my eye came to rest upon a suitcase I had taken to Paris ten days earlier. It was a natty thing in canvas and leather, part of the bathroom stash, and so covetable that I had borrowed it for my trip – bringing back in it two framed drawings: one by Epstein that Yvonne ffrench later sold to Henry Moore, the other an evocative and beautiful view of a nineteenth-century Paris shop front that is still in my possession. Suddenly alarm bells rang in my mind. My eyes bulged and then closed in horror, I yelped an expletive, and leapt dripping from the bath to grab the suitcase. Opening it was like being doused with the effluent from a sewer. From the gathered-silk 'oddments' compartment in the inside lid of the suitcase I extracted one of those circular wooden boxes the French sell their cheeses in. This was no puny brie, however, but a huge and grossly over-ripe Vacherin. It was literally pulsating with gases. Flinging on my clothes, I peered round the door to see that Miss Hall was not in sight, grabbed a plastic shopping bag, stuffed the cheese inside, and fled to South Kensington, where I dumped the bag and cheese into a dustbin.

Next morning Miss Hall knocked on the door, a thankful smile on her face. 'The horrid smell has gone, sir. Mr Fleming is really pleased.' In the afternoon, the men from the council returned to fill in the excavation. I thanked them and gave them Ronald's five-shilling tip 'for being so helpful'. I did think of pocketing it, for I felt that the men who had examined the bathroom ought to have followed their noses. In 1954, five shillings was the price of a good architectural drawing.

17

Boiling for Bryant

I T WAS IN 1954 or 1955 that I met Gilbert Ernest Bryant, of the celebrated and notorious Bryant Country House Index, introduced by either Jim Lees-Milne or Derek Sherborn – I think the latter. 'You must become a Boiler,' insisted Derek. I had heard of Gilbert from Rupert Gunnis and Howard Colvin, whose refrain was, 'He has a huge index of country houses'; but Jim was dismissive: 'He's like one of those train spotters' – as indeed he was, spotting and collecting country houses. (Jim's country-house indexing was of a quite different order.)

'Come for dinner, a little early,' Gilbert said, in the most friendly way, 'and I will teach you to Boil.' In Rivermead Court, an Edwardian mansion block at Hurlingham, the door of the flat opened to a man aged seventy-eight, with a soft rubicund face, and a shock of curly white hair. He was dressed in grey trousers, tweed jacket, and a frayed white shirt with an old school tie. He had just come from a meeting at the Natural History Museum, where he had spent most of his life, when not 'in the field' in Borneo, Java and Sarawak, as a world expert on beetles. J.W.T. Tapp, his younger coleopterist friend, tells me that Gilbert presented a total of 55,000 specimens to the Museum. He was also an authority on Liverpool tiles and Chelsea porcelain, and author of *Chelsea Porcelain Toys* (1925). Entymology encourages the classification and listing of species, and I suspect this was what lay behind Gilbert's impulse to collect the names of country houses – not pinned spreadeagled in specimen cases, like beetles, but written out on index cards and neatly arranged in boxes.

I think Byrne, Gilbert's Irish housekeeper, had died by 1955 – I do not recollect her presence at the many dinners and teas with macaroons that followed my first visit to the meeting-place of the Bryant Boilers, who included Derek, Bernard Pardoe, Michael Trinick, Peter Reid, and Hugh Weldon, the last a Marlborough College House Master who taught geography. Gilbert's flat was an exemplar of the ubiquitous 'brown style', whether oak, walnut or mahogany. There was not one iota of *goût*: all was redolent of a conservative family whose prosperity derived from Bryant & May matches. It was what might be described as 'comfortable-conventional', with a few fine pieces of Georgian furniture and porcelain, and framed groups of pretty grey and pale mauve Liverpool tiles. His books were all so tidily arranged in glazed bookcases that I found myself wondering, rather maliciously, if they were ever consulted.

A glass of sherry was the predictable preliminary to the invitation I had been waiting for: 'Let's go and see the Index. I'll show you how to Boil after dinner,' he added. What met my gaze were at least a hundred cardboard file-boxes, of such variety of hue as Joseph's many-coloured coat but all the right size for six-inch by four-inch cards. I pulled out one drawer, to find the cards so tightly packed that there was hardly room for another. Under Castle Ashby – chosen at whim – was a wodge of about sixty cards. The information on them was haphazard and repetitive, the visual evidence was a mixture of photographs and – what made the bile rise in my throat – engravings, cut down as necessary to fit the six-by-four format. It was horrifying to pull out mutilated engravings from Neale's *Seats of Noblemen and Gentlemen*, Angus's *Seats*, Harrison's *Seats*, Watts's *Views*, the rare *Polite Repository*, all similarly reduced. With those Castle Ashby cards in my hand, I began to understand what was meant by the term 'Boiling': it was to take all the cards for one house and see how the information could be condensed onto fewer. Even at this my baptism into the Bryant Index, I could sense the element of manic obsession. Since the war Gilbert had been putting onto his cards every single snippet of information about country houses and their inhabitants past and present that came his way, down to the place of decease of a member of a landed family, despite the fact that the house they died in was perhaps merely a nursing home! His intention was to record every known country house and every possible detail of the continuum of ownership or occupation – every fire, burglary, demolition, alteration, every incident, however trivial. The sheer scale of it was awesome.

Dinner was always roast chicken or a leg of lamb, with beer rather than wine, the conversation always country house gossip and the vicissitudes of county families. There were curious lapses or lacunae – for example, when I told Gilbert about my excursions to the houses around Stoke and Fulmer with Uncle Sid on his fishing and upholstery forays, he omitted to tell me that his family had owned Stoke Park in Buckinghamshire. There were constant grumbles in which the epithet 'brute' or 'bolshie' was used to describe demolition contractors, grumbles at the dismal failure of the National Buildings Record to cope photographically with the country house crisis. Derek Sherborn always came in for much praise as a stalwart opponent, in his government department, of the infernal bureaucracy that led to the failure to record doomed houses, but the NBR's Director, Cecil Farthing, was 'a brute'.

My enthusiasm for Boiling, and indeed for Gilbert's Index, cooled rapidly, a process accelerated after I joined the RIBA Library in 1956. I then discovered Howard Colvin's index, a precision tool of scholarly architectural documentation. I began to identify Gilbert's irritating deficiencies, not the least of which was his persistent failure to provide authority for his sources. My Boiling days ended, and as Gilbert grew older (he died in March 1965) he attended less and less to the monstrous albatross he had created.

He tried to gift the Index to an appropriate home but was brusquely rebuffed first by Cecil Farthing on behalf of the National Buildings Record, then by the Georgian Group: his demand that someone be appointed to work on the Index one day a week was simply unacceptable. In the end it passed by bequest jointly to Michael Trinick and Hugh Weldon, and I think Trinick then sold his share to Weldon. After Weldon's death in 1983 it became the Wandering Index and eventually, by way of the College of Arms, ended up in the Duke of Norfolk's library in Arundel Castle, where his Grace's Honorary Librarian, the architectural historian John Martin Robinson, pretends to Boil merrily one day a week. A while ago John (whom we affectionately call 'Mentmore' in commemoration of his – and our – failure to save that great house with its collections for the nation) told me of a violent nightmare he had had, in which he took the boxes containing the Index to the highest tower in the castle and cast all two million cards to the winds over the town of Arundel, like confetti. He awoke sweating.

18

Madame Vicaire

H E CAME IN to Collin and Winslow in mid 1954: dark hair, somewhat tousled, pointed nose in a sharp face, bright eyes, brick-red corduroy trousers with a tartan shirt and a brown tweed jacket. He was David Vicary. He snooped the shop thoroughly, and in the back room he was taken by a length of old green flowered damask, from Eywood, I think. I had been reading Christopher Hussey's *The Picturesque* (1927), and it lay open on a table. It initiated our friendship. He started to enthuse about Sir Uvedale Price's estate at Foxley, which he had discovered soon after that house had been demolished in 1947, so that we immediately found a common cause in abandoned country houses. As he left, he said, 'Come and have a drink this evening.' When I reported the sale of the damask and our conversation to Geoffrey Houghton Brown his comment was: 'Very clever young man, influenced by John Fowler. Lives above my friend Roy de Maistre, the painter.'

That evening I arrived at 13 Eccleston Street, where I was struck by David's natural flair for the juxtaposition of furniture, decorative objects, picture frames, fabrics. Even the contents of his kitchen were an artistic composition, yet nothing shouted 'decorator', or 'designed'. It seemed artless, although in fact it was the contrived outcome of his highly developed aesthetic sensibility. What was he, I wondered? Architect? Decorator? Garden designer? As I gradually discovered, he had been born in 1926, served in the Navy during the war, studied art at Salisbury Art College and architecture at the Regent's Street Polytechnic. He worked first in Dennis Lennon's office – he described this as his '*moderne*' phase – then for Alan Gore of Spencer & Gore, and was later associated with Vernon Gibbard. Gore sacked him for designing and building, without consultation, a mad pair of gates said to have been forty feet tall. Vernon claims he pinched all Gore's kitchen designs, which may well be true, for by 1960 David was in demand as a designer of kitchens in the 'tile and copper hood' style. Yet nearly all led to complaints and recriminations, of which those regarding Neville Conrad's kitchen in Manchester Square were typical: 'You have caused us more frustration, aggravation and annoyance than the entire job. I will sue for compensation.' This became a constant refrain, from client after client.

On 30 September 1960 David's dairies record 'Leave Eccleston' – for a flat at 170 Brompton Road, above Robin de Beaumont's Gloria Antica antique shop. By then I had known David for six years, and had a suspicion that he did not really know himself. I certainly appreciated a fellow enthusiast. He went to see the grotto at St Giles's House in Dorset, and bubbled and fizzed with excitement and emotion, conveyed to all his friends by postcard and letter. When he returned from visiting the newly-restored China House at Dröttningham in 1967, his enthusiasm was coruscating – 'That *heavenly* colour in the Yellow Chinoiserie Room! You *must* just see it' (and indeed, John Fowler did). If he read about the baroque town of Lecce in

Architectural Review, off he would go, and we would all be deluged with a minute-by-minute chronology of description and sensation; it was the same when he visited the Désert de Retz in 1960, at my instigation. He was a natural communicator, and it may be that his influence lay not so much in his executed work as in the sparks he could ignite, verbally and in writing. His surviving drawings and designs reveal an extraordinarily fertile mind, although frankly he was a designer of his time, educated by the Festival of Britain and its designers in the 1950s, not least Hugh Casson and, in particular, Russell Page's gardens at Battersea. The Greats of today all mutter, 'Ah, DV, what a loss, what a tragedy, what a wasted genius.'

I don't think it is just hindsight that makes me think I recognized something manic, almost schizophrenic in his behaviour even then. He was quite dotty. Both mentally and physically he was here, there and everywhere. The antique dealer and decorator Geoffrey Bennison called him a Whirling Dervish. In 1954 his letters were reasonably legible, but by 1970, if not earlier, had become almost unreadable, from his use of initials or pseudonyms in referring to people, and of a form of incomprehensible shorthand, always relating a *staccato* series or concatenation of events. They curiously resembled the letters of his friend Jonathan Vickers, who also went barmy and also possessed exquisite taste. I wonder if this should be a recognized mental condition, akin to a split personality.

In 1956 I found a book catalogue entry referring to a *Bibliographie Gastronomique* by one 'D. Vicaire' and sent it to Jonathan Vickers with a joking reference to David Vicary's reputation as a *dévoté* of *haute cuisine* involving the very richest ingredients (I introduced him to my own version of *pommes de terre dauphinoise*, made with lashings of double Jersey cream and known as Harris's Heart-stopper). Jonathan sent my card on to

David, and it came full circle in 2002 when I found both it and Vickers's letter quoted in David's diaries. It was what established his sobriquet 'Madame Vicaire', which Mariga Guinness was using in the 1960s and which, to his chagrin, stuck until his dying day.

Around 1970 I discovered from the legal advisor of the Royal Institute of British Architects that no other member or student member (as David was) in the long history of the Institute had been involved in so many disputes with clients. I already knew something about this because David and I had the same solicitor. A common trick of David's was to bill a client twice for the same job, and then try to take him to court in the teeth of evidence that the bill had been paid. One client in Wiltshire paid for a hundred and sixty-two rose bushes in a garden designed by David, only to find (by counting them) that a mere sixty had been planted. David was also very apt to invent a debt where no debt existed. It seems there was a mildly criminal edge to his dottiness.

Having spent four years with Doge Andrea Gritti, in 1958 I left 20 Thurloe Square to move on briefly to Jack Woods-Palmer's house in Alwyne Villas, Canonbury. The romantic outlook from my attic room onto Cyril Connolly's long garden with its ancient trees and Georgian gazebo was rudely compromised when, emerging from my room one morning, I found a huge glistening black naked figure in front of the mirror, masturbating into my bathroom basin. Jack's only comment was: 'Picked him up at The Angel. He's escaped from prison.' It seemed he was known as 'Blue Flash', from the enormity of what he possessed. Since this sort of thing was obviously going to be all too common, I was pleased when David offered me the attic studio room at 13 Eccleston Street, a house originally occupied by the sculptor Sir Francis Chantrey. The sandwich of tenants comprised Roy de Maistre on the ground floor, David at the top, and Mrs Augustine Courtauld, soon to become Rab Butler's second wife, in between. Rab would arrive there after dinner in his Rolls, and would pantingly depart down the creaking stairs at about two in the morning.

My friendship with David soon turned sour. Even then he was up to his tricks, and I found myself fending off creditors and paying his household bills as engineers arrived to cut off water, gas or electricity. The telephone bill was never paid. As his creditors pressed the bell incessantly I would lean out over the parapet to shout down, 'No access. Mr Vicary's away.' He was now in *my* debt. I sighed with relief when the RIBA seconded me to Columbia University in New York for six months. 'I'd move everything out,' our solicitor advised, and added, laughing, 'I warn you: he'll get you.' He did. When I returned in May 1960, having married Eileen, I found two obelisks and an ormolu lamp missing, and probably other items too. This was unsettling. The lamp was discovered in his bedroom, and when he claimed I had given it to him, I decamped.

The *coup de théâtre* and débâcle that followed had their genesis in David's diary entry for 8 July 1964: 'Bought L. Burrell Rectory £9,900.' This was the parsonage at Langley Burrell near Chippenham, made famous by William Plomer's discovery and publication in the late 1930s of Francis Kilvert's *Diary 1870–79*. It was a perfectly unspoiled rustic Palladian villa dated 1739, its panelled rooms pristine in their original paint, and the hall boasting a magnificent barley-sugar stair. David, bidding against a brigadier at auction, paid a grossly inflated price for 1964. He handed over a cheque as deposit, rang his solicitor to arrange legal matters, and then (it is said) decamped with Mariga Guinness to Leningrad. He had not a bean in the bank. To avoid probable legal proceedings, his mother honoured his cheque by taking out a mortgage. There were more ructions when David failed to thank her, and refused to pay his legal fees. 'You owe me the money,' he told his solicitor, 'and in any case you're only a junior in the firm.' His long-suffering mother cut him out of her will.

How David managed to decorate and furnish Kilvert's Parsonage is a mystery, but until about 1970 it was perfection. His love of gardens and knowledge of plants ensured that flowers were always part of the *mise en scène*. In the kitchen, for example, different arrangements of porcelain, faience or Delft would be suitably enhanced by David's choice of flowers, such as blackish-mauve hellebores with cream-ware. Yet the Parsonage was doomed. David's clients were departing in droves, a water-tank in the roof burst, creditors were clamouring. Thus began my friend's slide into a personal hell.

So full of brilliant invention was David's mind that it seemed he could not cope with reality. His very account sheets were tortuous labyrinths of confusions and fantasies. Having avoided him for at least a year, in 1970 I suddenly received a postcard saying how much he had enjoyed meeting us in the public gardens in Palermo – where we had not been. Similarly, he once wrote of meeting us at the Dröttningholm Theatre in Sweden – which he never did. In 1972 he arrived unexpectedly at the RIBA Drawings Collection, to donate some architectural drawings, he said. I was not in and he whirled away in anger, claiming to have had an appointment. He had not made an appointment with me – nor did he have any drawings to give. In his business he was unable to distinguish between right and wrong, in his personal affairs between fact and fiction.

At Kilvert's Parsonage roof tiles were displaced, rainwater penetrated. The burst tank was never repaired, but in any case his water, like all the other services, had been cut off. Woodwork

15. Kilvert's Parsonage near Chippenham, Wiltshire, overwhelmed by brambles, February 1995

bulged and moved with dry rot and wet rot. Fungoid spores blos-
somed. Slowly, relentlessly, nature began to take over. Creepers
insidiously entered broken windows, turned corners and
climbed up pictures. Brambles and creepers strangled the house
to a height of six feet and more. Nature entered in, as did

16. Kilvert's Parsonage after cleansing, February 1995

burgling yobs from Chippenham. Ceilings collapsed onto his furniture, floors gave way. Decay advanced throughout the house like an unstoppable cancer. He lived even worse than a tramp, his companions dozens of feral cats, to all of which he gave names, such as 'Pleydell-Bouverie' or 'Stephen Tennant'. Thousands of empty cat food and baked-bean tins were piled high or arranged like pyramids in window recesses. Dead cats and rats, sodden plaster and mouldering fabrics made a layered and stinking mulch with mouldy newspapers, muscle-man magazines and copies of *Men Only*, sometimes as much as two feet deep, in every room, upon which, resting like flotsom or emerging like wreckage from a storm-tossed sea, were valuable and exquisite pieces of furniture: a red lacquer chinoiserie chair lurching at a distressingly drunken angle, a broken Gothick side table, legs uppermost, like an upturned turtle. Through all this he burrowed out passages and made refuges. As cats died, so he reverently placed each body in a shoe box for a kitty coffin, and lined them up on shelves in the basement, as in a mausoleum.

He was nuts. He retreated from the squalor to his car, parked beyond the cordon of brambles in a car graveyard, and slept wrapped in newspapers. Small wonder he suffered a serious heart attack. Unwrapped and stinking, he occasionally went to The Ivy in Chippenham, where the kindly owners Julian and Isobel Bannerman were long-suffering comforters, feeding him and allowing him to have a bath. Eileen and I encountered him from time to time, always alerted to his presence by his smell. At Sir John Summerson's memorial service at St James's, Piccadilly in December 1992, David sat down beside me. A woman sitting on his other side put her handkerchief to her nose and swiftly departed, to be replaced by a man who looked strangely across at me, then also moved elsewhere. The pong caught one in the back of the throat.

Something prevented me from ever snooping Kilvert's Parsonage, which I regret, but I encouraged Dr John Newton, who was at Sherborne School with David, to call on him. John returned to London strangely silent, unable to believe what he had seen. Christopher Gibbs, who went to the Parsonage after David's death at the behest of the Bannermans, to evaluate what furniture had survived in the house, was equally nonplussed. The top layers had by then been cleaned out by men wearing gas masks, yet he says he will never to his dying day forget the sight that greeted him.

The last evening of David's life was spent with the Bannermans, and late on the evening of 21 February 1995 he left for the Parsonage, barely fifteen minutes away. He had just filled up his car with petrol, and when he hit a tree on his drive, the car burst into flames. A neighbouring farmer who saw the light of the fire merely imagined a party with a bonfire and a winter barbecue. Let us hope 'Madame Vicaire' suffered another heart attack, for he was burnt to a crisp, identifiable only by his teeth. Julian Bannerman discovered one of my missing obelisks in the Parsonage.

19

Investigator and acquisitor

Sherborn of Fawns

IT WAS THE summer of 1955, and I had written to Rupert
Gunnis enquiring about Hall Place in Berkshire, inspired by a
printed catalogue of its library that included only three architectural books, of which two were by James Gibbs. The austere
brick house with its baroque plastered rooms appeared to be
Gibbsian, of the best sort, so I posed the question: 'Was Hall
Place designed by Gibbs?' It certainly looked like it, and the
landscape bore the signature of Gibb's gardener, Charles
Bridgeman. Rupert replied: 'Write to Derek Sherborn, one of
those Investigators. He's writing a book on Gibbs.' I did so, and
from Fawns Manor, Bedfont, Middlesex came a prompt and
warm invitation: 'Come for tea on Saturday. We'll see some
houses roundabouts.' I knew Bedfont from my youth, when
Uncle Sid and I often cycled across the market gardens that
covered what is now Heathrow Airport. Bedfont was *my*
Middlesex – but I did not know Fawns.

I soon learned a lot about the house, off the High Street, near
the shops, and presenting to the public a façade plastered over in
the 1880s in Tall's patent concrete by a surveyor ancestor of

Derek's, William Sherborn, who had learnt his trade in Portugal. Patent concrete was not quite 'the true rust of the Barons' Wars', as Derek jovially pretended, nor indeed was Fawns really the ancient seat of the Sherborns of Bedfont, who had fought in those wars in the 1330s. The family had first leased it in 1648, and eventually bought it from the Duke of St Albans in 1806. But it matters not. Who is one to disabuse a friend of dreams of antique lineage? What mattered was that Derek was a fellow enthusiast for the architectural history and genealogy of landed possession, and a specialist in Gibbs and demolished houses. He became an Investigator in the Historic Buildings section of the Ministry of Town and Country Planning in 1948, a pioneer in the listing of historic buildings, and companion on many of the adventures recounted in *No Voice from the Hall*.

He is now one of my friends of longest standing in 'the trade' – but at this first meeting, there he was at the door of Fawns: tall, conventionally tweedy in a beige check jacket, with a soft round white face, welcoming me in his high-pitched flutey voice (it became squeaky when he was excited, as I later discovered). I was briefly introduced to his mother, obviously adoring, her face long and gothic. I found out soon enough that Mrs Sherborn was there to serve, and not be seen too often. She would appear when summoned, lay a scrumptious tea, then glide noiselessly away to the back parts of the house. Perhaps it was as well.

Fawns probably started life as a medieval hall house, but had suffered from the attentions of subsequent owners. Walls and ceilings seemed to press in upon one, and awkward corners and angles threatened claustrophobia. Cobwebs and dust-dirty gloom-inducing windows bespoke a continuity of ancient possession, adding romance to Derek's amazing collections. I soon came to realize that Derek and Rupert were adversaries in the Great Game of Acquisition. As a denizen of Thurloe Square I was familiar with the auction rooms of Robinson & Foster in Harrington Gardens, as was Derek, for at that time the National Buildings Record was just around the corner (not in Swindon, so recently described as a 'cultural desert' and the most hideous newer town in Britain). Derek and I met frequently. Derek was both Investigator and Acquisitor: his work in those dreadful years between 1948 and 1960 took him all over the country and he was able to combine listing with visits to antique shops and country house auctions, of which there seemed to be one every day. So the treasures accumulated in the noble seat. On that first visit to Fawns I noticed a Stubbs of John Wastell, a Soest of Nicholas Young (one of Wren's master-masons), a Dance of Capability Brown (bought at Robinson & Foster for thirty-five shillings), a portrait of Gibbs painted for his first patron the Earl of Mar, a Beechy of Master Brooks as St John the Baptist, and a Reynolds of William Dawtrey. Furniture was mostly fine-quality Regency, set off by ormolu ornaments, those popular lamp-bearing plaster Vestals by Thomas Hopper, or pairs of gilt candlesticks. Regency too were the many busts by Behnes and others, all cast-offs from the nobility and, I am sure, acquired in competition with Rupert.

'We're going to see the King of Iraq at Stanwell Place,' said Derek, tongue in cheek. (The king had bought Stanwell in 1948; it was sold following his assassination in 1958, and the house was demolished in 1959.) We arrived at the main entrance lodge and gates: what gates they were! Tall inner and lower outer piers supported the richest stone urns, designed by Gibbs and probably carved by J.M. Rysbrack. Gibbs was here with his gardener-crony Charles Bridgeman. 'I *told* Pevsner,' complained Derek, 'but he never turned the corner from the church.' Nikolaus was never one for crawling under barbed-wire fences, however, and this part was well wired in.

17. James Gibbs's gate piers at Stanwell Place, in what was once Middlesex but is now Surrey (photo: Derek Sherborn, 1950s)

We found ourselves in a decaying demesne, the sense of its abandonment heightened by the feelings always aroused when invading someone's privacy. We recognized the ghost of a formal layout by Gibbs and Bridgeman, designed for Richard Phillips, Governor of Nova Scotia. It must have been an extraordinary water garden, its park surrounded on two sides by canals fed from the river Colne and the Longford River. Other canals struck through a formal plantation, and to the south was yet another canal, naturalized into a lake. We spied the rusticated bridge with a mask keystone, quite likely by Gibbs, and found a large stone base Derek said had carried a pyramid. 'My grandfather could remember it,' he claimed. We followed the course of a serpentine channel to a cascade with a collapsed pediment and beside it a tall shaft-like banqueting house, in total ruin. Continuing along the water-course, a pile of rusticated stone stimulated speculation. Derek thought it a hermitage, of the Dido's Cave sort built at Stowe. The channel led us to a small wood bounded by a ha-ha, and here lying on the ground was the carved tympanum to a pediment. Derek bewailed the fact that he had, unsuccessfully, offered the caretaker in the lodge twenty-five pounds to turn a blind eye to its removal. Obviously what we were seeing was what had survived of a perfect small-scale semi-formal garden layout.

Derek explained that the attribution to Gibbs came from a manuscript memoir now in Sir John Soane's Museum. He also claimed that a caretaker had once shown him a photograph album belonging to the king in which were shown two richly carved plaster and gilt rooms in Gibbs' style – rooms later redecorated to the king's taste by the London firm of Mewes and Davies. After fifty years, Derek is still looking for this album. Who, apart from the dead king, would know where it is? Years later I found a drawing made by Thomas Robins in the 1750s, showing an old Bridgeman avenue, the naturalized lake, and a circular tree seat. It inspired me to return, which I did in the 1970s, and wished I hadn't: the effluvium of Heathrow by then was such that factories lapped its perimeter.

The fate of Stanwell and a hundred other similarly endangered houses eventually led to a falling-out between Derek and his civil servant bosses. His request to Cecil Farthing that he order statutory photographic records to be made was ignored, as were so many others in similar vein. The civil service certainly could not match and it seemed could not even tolerate Derek's enthusiasms. As a result the relationship deteriorated into vitriol, and eventually led to Derek's retirement without any of the honours he might have expected and that he so richly deserved as a pioneer Investigator.

After our visit to Stanwell we returned to Fawns for tea, sandwiches and cake, provided by Derek's attentive mother. Fawns saw me often, and Eileen too after 1960. We became used to unpleasant surprises. We observed Bedfont changing for the worse as the seat of the Sherborns grew ever more sullied by the proximity of Heathrow Airport. Derek stoutly stayed on, so gentle, so trusting, blind to the potential danger of the rough trade that passed his way, unconscious even of the malignity of a lodger who treated him ill. I recall one typical summer evening's dinner party by the swimming-pool, hidden from the prying eyes of village yobs who yearned to peek over the high wooden fence and join in the fun. This was no ornamental Georgian plunge-bath and the guardians of the place were not statues by van Nost but lithe, live gods cavorting in splashing water. Sausages sizzled on the barbecue, regularly replenished by Derek's mother, who would appear like a wraith, apparently oblivious of the male nudity surrounding her. 'What on earth can she make of all this?' muttered Eileen, turning to me in her deck-chair. 'You don't know these men's mums,' I replied. Derek suffered no fewer than twelve burglaries. His pride in his possession of his antique seat was great, but not great enough to outweigh an armed robbery in which a gun was put to his head and he was tied up. He survived by persuading his captors that a noise upstairs was a ghost: they fled. In 1983, his mother having long since died, it was time to depart – to Brighton.

20

At 66 Portland Place

IN MARCH 1956 I answered a knock on the door of my basement at 20 Thurloe Square to reveal Jim Lees-Milne in a waft of the Old Spice after-shave lotion we both used. He had just lunched with Jimmy (J.C.) Palmes, Librarian at the Royal Institute of British Architects. 'I'm sure you're intended to be an architectural historian, not an antique dealer,' he announced, and followed this up with Jimmy's offer to meet me to discuss a job he had in mind. The RIBA Library at 66 Portland Place, comprising both books and drawings, needed an assistant. I duly met Jimmy, who wrote to the other Jim that I was 'scruffy', but would do. So in May 1956 I joined the Institute – and only left it thirty years later.

The next watershed came in 1959, when Sir John Summerson, Curator of Sir John Soane's Museum, suggested to Eileen Spiegel of Columbia University in New York, writing her doctorate on 'Architectural Designs and Model Farm Buildings', that she should meet John Harris – though in fact our meeting did not depend on this suggestion. The summer of 1959 was gloriously hot; I was touring Lincolnshire for Pevsner's 'Buildings of England' series, and bumped into Eileen quite by chance in the

18. John and Eileen in a lost Austrian garden, 1968

Victoria and Albert Museum, where I was looking at architectural drawings of Swinstead House in Lincolnshire and had also, like her, applied to examine the engravings of Jean-Louis Le Rouge's *Jardins Anglo-Chinois*. However, it was not our common interest in Le Rouge that initially attracted me, but Eileen's efficient handling of her Praktica camera. Fate then decreed that her return to Columbia University should coincide with my secondment from the RIBA later in 1959 to the Avery Architectural Library of that University, and we married in New York in 1960. After that life was different, a co-operative adventure. After a little tuition my wife became peculiarly adept at snooping. She was first put to the test, perched precariously on the back of my Lambretta, at Lord Gainsborough's Exton Hall in Rutland, where we surreptitiously photographed the sadly ruined rotunda temple built of thatch with bark-covered columns.

21

A Duveen fabrication

IN 1959, THE world's two great architectural libraries were the Banister Fletcher Library of the RIBA and the Avery Architectural Library of Columbia University, New York. I persuaded my boss at the RIBA, Jimmy Palmes, to release me to Avery for six months, and this was the catalyst that led to my *Catalogue of British Drawings for Architecture, Decoration, Sculpture and Landscape Gardening in American Collections* of 1971. I also discovered new friends, not least that doyen of American architectural history, Henry Russell Hitchcock, and Adolf Placzek, soon to succeed Jim Vanderpool as Avery Librarian.

I never discovered how Thomas C. Howe, Director of the Legion of Honor Museum in San Francisco, knew of my whereabouts early in 1960, but he did, and set in train this tale of duplicity and deceit. He telephoned: 'We have a donor who wants to give us an English room. Duveen's have one in New York. Looks very good. By Sir William Chambers. From Sudbury Hall, Derbyshire. Would you go and report for us?' 'Of course,' I replied. Then he added, more pressingly: 'A decision is urgent as our donor likes the room.' I ruminated upon the various elements: 'Chambers . . . Sudbury in *Derbyshire*? Maybe Sudbury in Suffolk?' I consulted Howard Colvin's *Biographical Dictionary of English Architects* (1954) and found no record of Chambers having worked at either Sudbury.

The next morning found me in Duveen's New York warehouse, where Mr Edward Fowles told me the room had recently entered stock. He was enthusiastic: 'It's one of the finest we've ever had. There's a real demand for rooms like this.' Even then, when my knowledge of the subject was hardly more than youthful, I muttered to myself, 'Oh yeah!' At this time period room installations in American museums were not examined for authenticity in the way that paintings and other works of art were; already my scrutiny of such rooms, though brief, had filled me with reservations.

The panels of the room were propped up against the wall. I could not conceive how it could ever have been ascribed to the neo-classical Chambers. It was evidently English, but of earlier vintage, oak, with giant pilasters, and a chimney with overmantel. A curious feature was the panelling between the windows, carved to represent a Tree of Jesse, with brackets at the intersections of the branches to support porcelain – a rococo element, if ever there was one. My first impression was of a room dating between 1730 and 1740. I scrutinized it minutely. The door was on one long side, central and opposite the chimney-piece. This oddity worried me, for it was not usual for a room to be entered from a grand door on the long wall to face the chimney-piece in this way. It was a good room, yet something about it niggled and teased. I could not identify what it was, exactly, but instinctively I felt that something was not right. I returned to Avery to do some book investigations.

Next morning Thomas Howe rang me agitatedly, having spoken to Duveen's. His donor was pressing. What was my recommendation? I disabused him about Chambers, admitted that it was nevertheless a fine room, albeit earlier than suggested, and commented, 'I suppose it depends on what you have available to furnish it.' I confessed also to a nagging doubt, and said I felt I should return for a further look. Howe hissed with annoyance, and urged me to ring him the next day. I took against him, suspecting with fair confidence that he had already committed himself to the acquisition.

Mr Fowles was irritated when I returned, demanding to see the back of the panelling. Assistants had to be summoned to turn the panels around. I could not fault it: if it *had* been 'antiqued up', it was most convincing. Yet that damned central door perturbed me, for the room was clearly not a hall (the only possible explanation for the position of the door) but a saloon or drawing room. I spent the rest of the day in Avery Library, looking through books on English interiors, finding nothing. Going to one of the library bays for a book just before closing time, I found a pretty girl examining a pile of brochures. As I passed behind her I gave a sudden yelp and stood transfixed: there was the Sudbury room – the Tree of Jesse, at least, and the chimney-piece. I quickly explained myself lest the startled girl shout for protection against an obvious lunatic. She was studying the art trade, and had pulled this catalogue, issued by White, Allom, Lord Duveen's favourite firm of decorators, off the shelves quite fortuitously.

From the text of the catalogue, which the library had dated '*c.* 1925', it was clear that the room had come to Duveen's house in Kensington Palace Gardens, supposedly from a house near Sudbury in Suffolk. But Duveen himself had died in 1939, so at the very least it looked as though Mr Fowles had been guilty of an inaccuracy when he told me the room had 'recently' entered stock. All I could tell Howe was that the room was not what it purported to be but had apparently been convincingly cobbled together from various disparate elements. Miffed, he rejected it. I long wondered what happened to that room. I received no reply from Duveen's, nor to my claim for a fee from the wretched Howe.

I began writing this tale before a visit in the Spring of 2001 to Los Angeles, where the new Getty Museum holds the archives of three great dealers, Carlhian & Cie, French & Co., and Duveen. Teresa Morales, my research assistant there, directed me to Box 466, Folder #5 in the Duveen Papers, for the correspondence I wanted. But she had more to add: in the French & Co. papers she had found documents for the purchase of a 'Sir William Chambers Sudbury Room' from Mr Norton Simon in the summer of 1968. This was amazing. It must be the same room – but what was it doing with Norton Simon? The coincidences multiplied, for in the carrel or study bay next to Teresa's in the Getty library was Gloria Williams, a curator at the Norton Simon Museum of Art in California. She too made enquiries, and eventually produced documents for the sale of the room by Duveen's to Norton Simon on 15 March 1965. The room was never installed by Norton Simon but was sold on to Robert Samuels of French & Co. in 1968. Almost immediately, Samuels in his turn attempted to sell the room to the Los Angeles County Museum of Art; the letter of rejection from their Deputy Director, dated 12 August 1968, is couched in such a way as to imply that he suspected a fabrication.

More remarkably still, the correspondence in Box 466, Folder #5 revealed that Lord Duveen had first bought the room (for $22,000) for his house at 91st Street, New York, probably in the early 1920s. He never installed it there, but put it into his house in Kensington Palace Gardens. By 1928 it had been removed to

White, Allom's showrooms, and by the early 1930s was on Duveen's trade inventory. They had tried to sell it in 1951, then made a first offer to the Legion of Honor Museum in 1954. It was offered to Louisiana State University at Baton Rouge in 1959, to Blairman's in London in 1962 following the Legion of Honor offer, and so to Norton Simon in 1965. Where has it been since its sale to French & Co. in 1968, I wonder? But then, where is the famous Elizabethan long gallery from Albyns in Essex, or the great Restoration staircase from Coombe Abbey in Warwickshire, both bought by William Randolph Hearst? Where is the Palladian long gallery from Ashley Park, for years stored in French & Co's Long Island warehouse and seen there by me in 1970?

I was still fairly innocent in 1960, but discovered soon enough how common fabrications like the 'Sir William Chambers Sudbury Room' had once been; as I later wrote, in the matter of dealer as supplier of period rooms versus directors or trustees of museums, it was a case of 'Dealer Rules'. Happily, that can now be changed to the past tense – 'Dealer Ruled' – for such blatant practices are now largely a thing of the past.

22

Dodd as Cockerell

I T MUST HAVE been in 1959 that Eugene Dodd, a student of architectural history from Boston, first visited the Library of the Royal Institute of British Architects. It became his second home, his face familiar to us all. He and I got together when I discovered he was writing his doctoral thesis on C.R. Cockerell. My first impression of him never altered: shortish, somewhat pointed face, blue eyes, hair brushed back flat Brylcreem style, shabby dark suit shiny with wear. He was always dressed formally, with a tie of course, often with a stiff collar: I never saw him in casual attire. In retrospect I suppose he was Boston Brahminish, but it did not occur to me at the time, for he behaved as though he was genteelly impoverished. Many of us in the Library helped him along in small ways, paying for his taxis, entertaining him to lunch and dinner. Once, on his birthday, I gave him a copy of Nicholas Revett's *Antiquities of Ionia* in the original edition of 1769.

Dodd worked with manic obsession, advised by John Summerson and Nikolaus Pevsner. Never did they extol a pupil more. Praise tripped off their tongues – 'brilliant', 'genius', 'a born writer'. After four years the praise had not dulled, although both were concerned that he had not finished his thesis, intended for submission in 1963. Nevertheless, they were patient, recognizing the genius in Dodd, who had, so they believed, penetrated Cockerell's very mind. So elegant was his writing, so descriptive and analytical, that any exception could and should be made. 'Never have I read architectural history of such quality and distinction,' said Pevsner. 'It will be worth waiting for.'

Poor Dodd! His father died, and he was forced to go home to his house near Boston, a place called Assebet Hills Orchards. He promised to return, and did so about six months later. Then tragedy struck again: his mother died too, and Dodd left England and his Cockerell studies for ever. I lunched with Pevsner and Summerson, and they bemoaned his loss to British architectural history.

Then, in 1966 or 1967, Eileen and I were heading down the steps of the Metropolitan Museum of Art in New York to catch the bus for The Cloisters, the Museum's out-station some miles uptown, when there was Dodd. 'Gene!' I cried. 'Hullo! This is great. Where have you been?' Pleasantries followed, and Dodd agreed to come to The Cloisters with us. We didn't make much of his obvious irritation at the slowness of the bus (indeed, at being *on* the bus), but we did muse a little when he mentioned that he was staying at the Biltmore, a luxury hotel. That evening we met him 'under the clock' there, and took the subway downtown to dinner. He seemed annoyed at all the people around him and then, as we approached the restaurant, surprised us by suddenly confessing to feeling unwell, apologized, and literally disappeared round a corner. We ascribed this to an eccentricity perhaps to be expected of 'that poor boy who had lost both his parents so early'. Next day he rang to apologize again, with renewed expressions of friendship, and offered to take us on a tour of New England museums. He knew that we were on our way to stay with friends in Farmington, Connecticut, where we were to lunch with Wilmarth Sheldon Lewis and see his collection of Walpoleana.

Matters came to a head at the Wadsworth Athenaeum in Hartford, Connecticut. He hurried out, having forgotten to feed the parking meter, and returned with a face black as thunder at getting a ticket. 'It's our fault,' I said, and gave him a few dollars, at which he announced: 'We must leave now. I'll drop you in Farmington.' The ensuing silences were oppressive, and at a turning just outside Farmington he drew off the main road and dumped us and our bag. 'Farmington's along there,' he exclaimed, pointing, and drove off. Nonplussed, we trudged on our way.

Whenever we encountered Pevsner, Dodd's name would surface in conversation. Pevsner's hopes had been raised by the fact that Dodd had asked him for a reference – he was applying for a senior position in the Art History department at the University of California at Berkeley. Few faculty chairmen can have received such glowing references as those from Pevsner and Summerson, and Dodd got the job against stiff and more mature competition. Pevsner was ecstatic. This would be just the fillip Dodd needed to finish his thesis and gain his doctorate. The last he had heard was that the thesis was only wanting its footnotes. Then rumours began to percolate from California: Dodd could not face a class of students. Eileen recollected the time he gave a talk on Cockerell to the RIBA Library Group: he was shaking and sweating in fright beforehand, but gave a brilliant lecture, literally as if Cockerell himself were speaking. Berkeley, it was learned, had sidelined Dodd into an editorial post. But not for long. Dodd disappeared.

Sometime around 1970 Eileen and I were in Boston having

drinks with an old Boston family. Suddenly remembering the name, I enquired idly about Assabet Hills Orchards. 'You mean the Dodd residence?' I was startled to discover that the family had owned large tracts of land in north Boston. Gene was described as 'an odd and rich fellow'. The mystery deepened.

I'm not sure when I first discovered that he had become Director of the Hancock Shaker Museum in Massachusetts, but when I was lecturing at Yale in 1972 I found a telephone number for him. I phoned. He was there and, surprisingly, agreed to come over to Newhaven, where we enjoyed a warm meeting. I remembered that Pevsner had implored me, should I ever meet Dodd, to convey his offer of help in completing the footnotes for his thesis – an astonishing affirmation of Pevsner's confidence in his student. 'Can't be done,' said Dodd. 'I've lost the thesis. Left the only copy with a book-binder. Can't remember who. Tell Pevsner I'm sorry.' I thought (but did not say) that it was curious he should only have one copy.

In any case, the problem was not insurmountable. London University possessed a list of recommended binders, and two telephone calls discovered a binder who said, in surprised tones, 'It's been on the shelf for nine years, awaiting the footnote section.' Pevsner was ecstatic and, as Dodd's advisor, immediately rushed along to collect the thesis.

The story now passes to the Isle of Anglesey, where I had discovered a huge and hitherto unknown archive of Cockerell family papers in the possession of Mrs Anne Crichton. It was at the time when David Watkin at Cambridge was writing his book on Cockerell (published in 1974; the Crichton collection was unknown to him, and he was able to take advantage of it). Mrs Crichton bade me down to Anglesey to examine her papers, and what a cache they proved to be, notably his diaries, precious documents running from 1821 to 1830. I had already skipped through Dodd's thesis in Pevsner's office, and recalled that he had quoted from the diaries extensively. 'I didn't realize you knew Dodd,' I said. Anne Crichton gave me a blank look. 'Dodd? Never heard of him. Take the diaries back to London. Perhaps this Dodd has discovered copies.'

Pevsner was shattered by my hints that the diary entries used by Dodd were fictitious: he had put all his faith in his favourite pupil. But fictitious they were. Nothing matched. Yet as I read each quote, comparing it with the undisputed original, I was overcome, not only by the sheer scale of the deception, but by Dodd's genius. The language was convincingly both of the period, and entirely Cockerell's in style and grammar.

In one entry Dodd had Cockerell leaving London from a named City inn by a named coach, stopping at an inn in Reading for breakfast, and arriving at Bristol to meet John Nash, who had come from the Harfords at nearby Blaise Castle. Cockerell then described how he had shown Nash his Bristol Literary and Philosophical Institution of 1821, and recorded Nash's observation that the circular rotunda at the angle had given him the solution to the problem of handling the angle of his church of All Souls in Langham Place, built from 1822. 'Aha!' said John Summerson to me later. 'I once suggested to Dodd that there might be a connection between these two buildings – and at our next session he produced the diary entry as confirmation. I thought it an odd coincidence at the time, but doubt quickly passed away.'

Other incidents then began to slot into place in this saga. The publisher Jock Murray had asked me about Dodd's work, as it was common knowledge that Dodd had located correspondence between Byron and Cockerell, when the latter was in Greece between 1810 and 1814. Where was it? Would the thesis tell? I looked – but of course, the footnotes were missing! Nor were the Acknowledgements (from which the quotations which follow come) helpful when it came to the location of manuscripts. Walter Ison denied any knowledge of 'the Cockerell drawings and manuscript grangerised in a volume in his possession'. Archivists in Copenhagen informed me that, as far as they could discover, the archives of Professor Johannes Broendsted, whose 'generosity and hospitality' had enabled Dodd 'to spend nearly three months in Copenhagen examining the Cockerell documents among the papers of his great-grandfather Peter Oluf Broendsted', did not exist. Jock Murray, whose enquiry had set my investigations in train, of course denied that there was any Cockerell correspondence held 'in the remarkable collection of Byroniana at 50 Albemarle Street'.

I went to the Cockerell correspondence files in the RIBA Drawings Collection to see what they could tell me about Cockerell and Dodd. I discovered that someone had razored articles about Cockerell out of some of the nineteenth-century periodicals held in the Library. Of course, this need not have been Dodd's doing; sadly, it was a too-common occurrence. As I read a few of Cockerell's letters, it began to dawn on me: *Dodd was Cockerell.* Even his handwriting was a mirror image of Cockerell's. 'That's interesting,' said Eileen. 'Some years ago I remember asking Gene how he had acquired his wonderful writing style, to which he replied, "I've read and memorized every word that Summerson wrote, so as to perfect and imitate his style."' He clearly did the same with Cockerell, and in imitating him he had *become* Cockerell. He was writing autobiographically.

There may be some who think Dodd perpetuated one of the most extraordinary architectural frauds of the century. I later sent Summerson a copy of Dodd's chapter on Wren and Cockerell, to which he replied briefly: 'Dear John, You are right about

Dodd. Yes, I always thought him a genius. He is the reincarnation of Cockerell. Yours ever, John Summerson.' Later, John recalled that a certain eminent Spanish historian had invented diaries 'written by' Velázquez, in order to carry and present his hypotheses.

There is one more enigma in this bizarre story, and a postscript. Because of the unreliability of Dodd's acknowledgements, mystery surrounds the provenance of some undisputed Cockerell drawings of the Elgin Marbles, loaned by Dodd to the late Jacob Rothenberg: they are supposed to have come from a 'Mrs Cockerell', whom neither I nor Professor Watkin has been able to trace. The date they bear – 1806 – seems not to be in Cockerell's hand, may have been tampered with, and in any case cannot be correct.

As for the postscript, Pevsner's library was bought by the Getty Center for the Humanities in California, and when I was browsing the shelves there in 1987, what should I find but Dodd's thesis! Many were the thoughts and memories evoked as I held it in my hands. My feelings for Gene had never been less than affectionate. Opening the thesis, I found attached to it a copy of a letter from Dodd with a Boston address, informing the Getty that anyone might use his thesis for their benefit. After much thought, I wrote Dodd a friendly letter, circumspectly suggesting that his thesis was such a good read, it could well be published as it stood. He never did reply, and he has now left Boston.

23

Jenkins' throttle

IN 1966 A spectacular collection of drawings by Colen Campbell (1676–1729) was discovered at Newby Hall and Studley Royal, bought from Henry Vyner, and presented to the RIBA by the Wates Foundation in 1967. At the end of his life Campbell had been working for John Aislabie of Studley Royal and had designed the stable block there, where Henry Vyner had latterly lived. The discovery of these drawings caused unprecedented excitement in architectural circles, for they transformed our understanding of this pioneering neo-Palladian architect. For Howard Stutchbury, however, their discovery could not have been more inopportune. The architectural community had long awaited a biography of Campbell, and Stutchbury's *The Architecture of Colen Campbell* was, at this critical moment, actually in the throes of being printed by the University of Manchester Press.

Something ought to be done, and urgently, I felt. Stutchbury was away on holiday (he was the City Architect of Bath), so I phoned the Press and spoke to his editor. 'Well, it's too late,' said he. 'We are into galley proofs.' I pleaded that the incorporation of a study of the drawings was essential, and was even bold enough to suggest that without it, the book would be regarded as inadequate: they should hold up the printing. The editor was testily adamant that the Press was not prepared to pay for revised galleys, but relented to the extent of agreeing to the addition of a short Appendix. I warned him Stutchbury's reputation as an architectural historian would suffer from his intransigence – as indeed it did, grievously.

I studiously refused to review the book, but the hovering Sword of Damocles represented by those newly discovered drawings of Campbell's fell in a now celebrated review in the *Times Literary Supplement*. Few authors of architectural biography have been so shredded! It was a total demolition job. *TLS* reviews were unsigned in those days, but to those in the know it could have been written by only one person: Dr Andor Gomme, of Keele University.

Stutchbury's doctoral advisor at Manchester University had been Frank Jenkins, a long-serving member of the RIBA's Library and Drawings Committee, and an officer of the Society of Architectural Historians. I soon picked up rumours of his violent reaction to the review. I knew Frank well as a professional colleague, and indeed he had generously agreed to supervise any thesis I might write should I decide to work for a degree in architectural history, so I was not surprised when the door of the Drawings Collection opened one day and he appeared. (Oddly enough, at that very moment I was examining a pile of Campbell drawings in preparation for my own RIBA catalogue.)

Our eyes met. Frank looked down at the Campbell drawings. His face was very red and strained, and there was a peculiar look in his eyes. He came nearer, and I was just about to suggest a cup of tea when, uttering a strangled cry, he suddenly lunged at me and grasped me about the neck screaming that Stutchbury had been his friend and best pupil, and my review was wicked and vicious. My secretary Bobbie leapt to my aid, trying to pull him away. He refused to let go, so I picked up Colvin's *Dictionary* and clonked him on the side of the head, shouting, 'I didn't write the bloody review!' He then fell over a stool, we pulled him up, and he left, shaking. He later resigned his RIBA appointments.

Recently I told this story to Andor Gomme. 'I've become milder as my years increase,' he observed. Having twice been the butt of his pen, I could only return his smile in disbelief. I dedicate this tale to him.

24

Of Blunt, alarms and MI5

THE DRAWINGS COLLECTION of the Royal Institute of British Architects moved from Portland Place to 21 Portman Square in 1970, and the Collection and Heinz Gallery were opened by HM The Queen in May 1972. A security system was installed, and I was the principal key-holder. Through 1972 and into 1973, I think, we were plagued by a rogue alarm. It must have gone off twenty times, for no apparent reason. I once asked myself why it never played its malevolent tricks at the weekend. It never did. My secretary thought it odd that the police were not more concerned. 'They usually read the riot act if an alarm misbehaves too often.' They never did. She added, 'Do you realize that it only ever goes off between two and four in the morning?' She had also observed that the security firm called out so regularly to reset it never complained.

Whenever there was an 'incident', my routine was usually the same: receive telephone alert, call taxi, hold it at Portman Square, turn off alarm, return home in taxi and to bed. The very first time it happened, a policeman was waiting at the door and we cautiously searched the building. Never again did one turn

124

up, except for one notable occasion when I arrived to find Portman Square ringed off by *dozens* of policemen: one of their fellows on the beat had been murdered in Portman Mews. I had to open up, and had the unpleasant task of accompanying armed police on a search of number 21.

Sometimes when I was called out in this way I would pay off the taxi and sleep on the office couch. If insomnia struck, there were always papers of no consequence to be shuffled about.

On one occasion I had paid off the taxi, but having dealt with the alarm decided to collect some papers and go home after all. I never bothered with lights on the stairs at night, for the great skylight above the stairwell admitted quite enough ambient light to see by. I was on the upper landing about to descend when I heard a familiar 'click', the sound of the front door being opened and then closed. I froze, caught my breath, and listened. There was a second 'click', as the door opened and closed again. Tiptoeing quickly but silently to the window looking onto Gloucester Place, I glimpsed two men hurrying across the road to a parked car. I frowned. Had I dreamt it? But that 'click' was so familiar. My secretary shrugged when I told her. Perhaps I had imagined it. Looking back, I recall two further curious incidents which were surely part of the puzzle, though I did not make the connection at the time.

I frequently worked late, and very often walked along Park Street to the old Holdernesse Hotel, where a convenient bar supplied excellent steak sandwiches, before taking the bus or tube home to South Kensington. On one such evening I noticed a man in Portman Street wearing a grey mac, and as I walked on it occured to me that I had seen him before, not once, but several times. He was fifty yards behind me when I suddenly changed my mind and my direction, having decided to give myself dinner at Harry's Bar in South Audley Street instead. Arriving there, I dithered again, thinking that after all I would go home. As I turned, there was the man in the grey mac hovering at the corner. Near Hyde Park underground station I noticed him turn away and cross the road behind me. It certainly seemed as though I was being followed, but I supposed that he was merely looking for a gay pick-up.

Then there was the curious case of the fire exit opening from 21 Portman Square onto Gloucester Place. It served both the RIBA Drawings Collection and the Courtauld Institute of Art, which occupied the basement and upper two floors of 21, with direct access from their main premises at number 20. We in the Drawings Collection noticed that someone was making exits via the back fire stairs, for we twice found the street door left open. It puzzled us. The Registrar at the Courtauld could offer no obvious explanation, except that a student might have got shut in and found that way out, unaware there was a caretaker.

Now, upstairs at number 20 the Courtauld's Director, Sir Anthony Blunt, had a flat, and I often enjoyed an after-work drink with him there. We had met by chance at a café in Lecce, when Anthony's tale of how the Courtauld could not afford to buy the lease of the whole of 21 Portman Square led to the decision to split it up, with my Collection making the middle of a delectable sandwich. Anyone could exit from number 20 via our stairs, and indeed Anthony's flat shared a party wall with a room at the top of number 21.

One of my assistants in the early 1970s was a young architectural historian named Johanna Symonds, who often used to stay late cataloguing the Voysey drawings. Recently she told me a tale that would be incredible, were it not that it adds another piece to the jigsaw. Her father, Ronald Symonds, was Deputy Director General of MI5 from 1972. It was he who had earlier concluded that Blunt, not Roger Hollis, was a Soviet mole, and negotiated the terms of Blunt's immunity from prosecution in 1964. In 1971 Symonds asked his daughter to lend him her door and alarm keys. At first she demurred, worried about what would happen if her bosses in Portland Place found out. Her father reassured her that they were 'already in the know' (although Patrick Harrison, the RIBA's Secretary, to this day denies it), and so she handed over the keys for copying.

A condition of his immunity had been Blunt's promise never again to get in touch with his Russian contacts. A watch put on number 20 after hours revealed that undesirables, Russian or otherwise (probably more of the latter than the former, in fact), entered number 20 at night, but were not always seen to leave again. The decision was therefore taken to bug Blunt's flat from number 21, the other side of the party wall. The necessary servicing or adjustment of these listening devices seems sometimes to have set off our alarms. The night I heard the door click and saw the two men, the engineers must have opened the front door, found the alarm turned off – indicating that someone was there – and hurriedly retreated. Johanna told me she subsequently learned from her father that whenever she left late she was followed by MI5 all the way to her fiancé's flat – there was a full record of all her arrivals and departures. It looks very much as though the man in the grey mac was not after all following me for my *beaux yeux*.

There is an appendix to this tale. Miranda Carter, Blunt's biographer, makes no reference at all to Francis Watson, who before the war had been Registrar at the Courtauld Institute of Art under its first director, W.G. Constable. He was the same age as Blunt and of the same vintage at Cambridge, and as Surveyor of The Queen's Works of Art was his colleague in the Royal Household. He occasionally popped over from the Wallace

Collection in Manchester Square for a drink, either in my office or in Blunt's flat. Privately, we agreed that Blunt was not charismatic. He might be ready enough to offer his knowledge to his students, but there was no sense of enthusiasm about him in private. Talking about this one evening at dinner with Francis and Jane, I observed that Blunt's face disclosed nothing – 'sphinx-like' was I think the phrase I used. 'I think he's got much to be enigmatic about,' Francis commented. I thought it a little odd that Francis never referred to Blunt's public exposure in 1979, merely expressing relief that he himself had avoided identification as another gay courtier in the artistic service of HM The Queen, and thus the attentions of journalists.

On 25 March 1983 Blunt telephoned me from his flat in Portsea Hall at about five in the afternoon. Would I come for a drink? He needed to speak to me, urgently. There was pleading in his voice. I simply had to decline, as Eileen and I had a dinner engagement out of London. 'I do promise to call you in the morning. Let's have coffee then,' I replied, sensing Anthony's disappointment. Next morning he was dead.

25

Sir Basil Spence

BEFORE I MET him, the architect Sir Basil Spence had been described to me as 'pompous' and 'pretentious'. I had long admired his Sussex University and Guards Barracks at Knightsbridge, thought him the first Post-Modernist of our era, and yearned to acquire his archive for the RIBA. It was only when I had to negotiate the gift of one of his drawings to commemorate the award to him of the RIBA's Royal Gold Medal that I met the great man. Those negotiations proved tedious, and the future of his archive was clearly *not* on the agenda. Very reluctantly he agreed to visit the Drawings Collection, and I prepared a delicious lunch. When he arrived and she enquired his name, the gentle receptionist was startled by his brusque 'Sir Basil Spence, Royal Gold Medallist'. She brought him upstairs. For half a minute he surveyed my room as if nonplussed that I should be housed in such splendour, and then observed, apropos nothing at all: 'You know, when I was building the Knightsbridge Barracks I had a private chat with the General Officer Commanding London District, who assured me that I was "one of them", and they would see that the Defence

Ministry brooked no objection to my tower on Hyde Park.' We had scarcely begun to discuss the sort of drawing it would be suitable for him to donate when I noticed him looking at his watch. He noticed me noticing, and said, 'I see you've someone to lunch. I'll be going.' I protested that it was he who was to be my guest. 'No, no,' he insisted, and marched out.

The matter of the Royal Gold Medal drawing dragged on and on. Eventually, a year or so later, a group of distinguished members of the RIBA Library Drawings Committee was invited to Spence's office at his house in Islington to discuss it. Similar invitations had twice been cancelled. This one was not, but the omens were hardly auspicious. The front door opened to reveal Sir Basil, with his goatee beard, who gave us a studied greeting, moving his head self-consciously to one side and glancing towards the bronze bust of himself by Epstein. The bust was raised high, artfully lit and backed with laurel, just like that of a Roman emperor. *Poseur*, we all thought.

There was desultory talk about his archive of drawings and a Basil Spence Room and the Epstein bust, but such a room would have to be fitted out to Spence's requirements by the RIBA, and before any gift was made, he insisted, a *catalogue raisonnée* of the drawings must be compiled and published. Then he turned off the subject. We stood about with our drinks – only sherry was on offer – Spence a little apart, as if on stage. 'Of course, I am the greatest architect in Britain,' he announced. We all gaped. Was this his way of telling us his drawings were too precious to be cared for by an institution such as ours? Then he suddenly changed the subject, and began to talk about his war experiences in Normandy as a tank officer. His eyes began to glisten. He really *was* on stage. He had twice been mentioned in despatches, but clearly could not forgive his senior officer for gaining the Military Cross. 'I was brave,' he explained. 'What I did that day deserved the Victoria Cross, and it was denied me, in favour of my commanding officer's MC.' Enthusiasm welling up, he enlarged upon his heroic encounter with German tanks. We were initially transfixed, then the war veteran J. Quentin Hughes, himself the holder of an MC, made his excuses and walked away, followed by S. Rowland Pearce. I too had had enough, and remembered a fictional engagement. Spence just nodded. He had totally forgotten the purpose of our visit. In the hall I naughtily unplugged the spot-light illuminating Epstein's bust, and dislodged the laurels.

26

The Indian Gibbs

MY COLLEAGUE IN architectural history Dr Terry Friedman published the standard biography of James Gibbs in 1984, and I used to delight in twitting him about all the country houses that might reasonably be attributed to Gibbs, but had found no place in his tome. His defence was that he wanted to treat only documented works, which was reasonable enough. One day when my staff and I and Gervase Jackson-Stops were enjoying a convivial and bibulous lunch, Terry's lack of a sense of humour became the subject of ribald conversation. 'Let's play a joke on him,' Gervase suggested.

Gervase's idea was that we might invent an unknown house by Gibbs. 'One in India, perhaps?' I suggested: I had recently been reading some correspondence in the Gloucestershire Record Office between John Freeman of Fawley Court and Governor Pitt of Fort St George on the subject of architecture. We put our heads together. Yes, something at Fort St George, we concluded. We rehearsed our lines. Andy, the Drawings Assistant, was convulsed with laughter, and the secretaries were 'ooh'-ing in feigned horror. 'Now I'll make the call. Keep straight faces. No giggling, anyone.' The phone rang in Terry's office in Leeds. 'Keep straight faces, keep straight faces,' I whispered, then assumed my best Indian accent: 'Ah yes, is that the Doctor Friedman? My name is Dr Sen Gupta.' A dour 'Yes.' 'Dr Friedman, we think you will be astounded by our discovery. My friend Benmali Sarkar is secretary of the Madras Tennis Club, of very ancient foundation. In archive, two years ago, he has found in a trunk papers of Governor Pitt of Fort St George.' Terry was breathing heavily by now, and yes-yessing.

Then Gervase/Sarkar intervened: 'Yes Sir Friedman, there are letters between Mr Freeman of a place called Fawley in 1730, a Director of your estimable East India Company. He tells Mr Pitt the honourable Governor about his friend, a name we think reads Jeebs.' There was a loud grunt from Terry. I continued, in my role as Gupta: 'Now, we poor scholars in Madras know nothing about an architect called Jeebs, but your most important book – oh, sir, it must have taken you a life to write. It is in our university, bought with your fine British Council funds. What excitement, Sir Doctor, and it is the same as your Gibbs!'

'What?' Terry was now panting audibly with excitement.

'Yes, Dr Friedman. The house for Sir Pitt is still in Madras. Oh! it is so fine, with those square stones on surface, what you call rusty-cation. We have found rolls of drawings, but we beg pardon, Sir, so mildewed, but fine ceiling shapes according to a Mr Bagette.'

There was an explosion of air down the phone. 'I can't believe this,' said Terry.

'Yes, yes, Doctor, and my Club wishes you to come out here. Will you, sir, will you? Mr Sarkar – he will be so your friend – has spoken to the American Express in Calcutta. We will be so honoured to pay your fare.' We could imagine poor Terry quivering with anticipation.

'When do you want me to come? This is incredible. It must be published,' he blurted out.

Alas, this finished us all, and amid our shrieks of uncontrollable laughter the phone went dead.

27

The rite of the annual
Pevsner dinner

A S I GREW through my adolescence as an architectural historian I increasingly saw Nikolaus Pevsner as an encouraging
mentor, despite my false start in his Penguin office. He had
pressed me to write for the *Architectural Review* and given me the
co-authorship of the *Lincolnshire* volume in the 'Buildings of
England' series, and although he was wary of me as a critic of his
methods in the production of that series, our relationship as professional colleagues was full of *bonhomie*. Eileen and I were social
and convivial, so dinners featured largely in our diary. Among
our first invitees were Nikolaus and Lola, and who better to
marry them up with than the Wolfgang Hermanns – both
couples being scholar-refugees from Nazi Germany. By the end
of the evening Eileen was wishing there had never been a beginning. It was an excruciating two and a half hours of tension, cautious eye-contact, interminable silences, and desperate invention
of subjects for conversation. In the kitchen Eileen muttered,
with tears in her eyes, 'Do they *hate* each other?'

A month later she met Wolfgang in the British Library. He took her aside and kindly remarked, 'Did you not realize that although I was Pevsner's best man, I have not spoken to him for twenty years?' He then explained: in 1940 Pevsner had dedicated his *Academies of Art, Past and Present* to 'W.P. in grateful and faithful remembrance of the past', and 'W.P.' was Wilhelm Pinder, Pevsner's 'master', but a man who had remained mute as his Jewish scholars and colleagues were expelled from their jobs. The dedication was regarded by German–Jewish refugees in England as at best misconceived, at the worst reprehensible. Among the German refugee community in England, both the Hermanns and the Wittkowers had lost relatives to the death camps by 1940.

Nikolaus was never any good at the unexpected. His course in whatever he was doing must be clearly charted out beforehand. In his travels for 'Buildings of England' he was never able to predict what might be 'on the other side of the hill' (*pace* Liddell Hart). His daily rota was so corseted that, by his own admission, it included the fourteen minutes in the Tube between Goodge Street station and Hampstead, allotted to working on the papers on his clip-board. So it was with his annual dinner parties. Eileen and I were once invited to dine at his flat in Hampstead, but intimate *ad hoc* dinners with a few friends were not the Pevsner style, being too time-consuming for one who habitually worked to an unalterable schedule. Better to satisfy his social obligations by once a year hosting half a dozen restaurant dinners for about twenty persons each.

Year by year Eileen and I gloomily anticipated The Dinner. It was not just the cuisine, which was often at best unexciting, but his bizarre selection of guests: never have we endured so many people we disliked and who, I imagine, disliked us. It was almost as if Nikolaus derived a perverse pleasure from bringing unsuitables together. He frequently took over the Isoken Restaurant in Wells Coates's Lawn Road Flats, a predictable choice for a Modernist. The ambience was Modern-Movement-dreary, the food excruciatingly plain and awful. For those of us who enjoyed good food in good company it was an annual torment, a combination of those we never wanted to meet with food we never wanted to eat. And how well we both recall a dinner he gave at a Hampstead Vale restaurant. It was not only our last, but also (as it turned out, and for reasons Nikolaus could not appreciate) the best.

We were to make our separate ways to this discomfiting evening, I by bus, Eileen by Tube. It was rush hour, and on arriving at Hampstead she found the lift crammed to capacity. The back of a head in front of her looked familiar: it was Nikolaus, holding a briefcase in one hand and his clip-board stuffed with papers in the other. The lift doors opened at the top, and suddenly there was a cry: NP had tripped on the edge of the lift floor and fallen on his knees, and was in danger of being trampled by the crowds. 'Nikolaus,' Eileen shouted, 'let me help. Give me your bag. We need you for dinner.' Up got Nikolaus, very shaken, but not too shaken to retort: 'What do you mean? You're not invited to dinner today.' To which Eileen resolutely replied, 'But I am! John's meeting me at the restaurant.' 'No, you're not,' contradicted Nikolaus, and then relented, '– but come along and have a drink.'

I was early at the rendezvous, already waiting when Nikolaus entered with Eileen and greeted me with a grin: 'You've got the wrong night.' I guiltily checked my diary, but there it was. Two more guests came through the door. Smiles on NP's face, forced smiles on ours. Then consternation when Hugh Casson came breezily in. Nikolaus gave a puzzled stare: he had not been invited. We conferred with Hugh, who in whispers agreed we'd get a better dinner round the corner. Nikolaus was now consulting his list. Three other guests followed, ticked off as OK, but when Ernst Gombrich arrived, incomprehension and horror suffused Nikolaus's face. So it was with Mark Girouard, with Ian and Elizabeth Nairn. I seem to recall a conspiratorial look about Elizabeth. A few more 'untouchables' came in. Nikolaus was furious by now, biting his nails, as was his habit. Where was this guest, where was that one? It was not his model of Germanic precision and efficiency.

Three hours later we left. Never had we enjoyed a more agreeable annual dinner, a more perfect mixture of guests. Nikolaus never discovered that Elizabeth, while doing a temporary secretarial stint in his office, had mischievously tinkered with the guest-list when sending out the invitations for that evening (her husband disliked these dinners as much as we did). We never discovered what Nikolaus thought was the reason why the people who turned up for this dinner did not tally with the names on his own list. As we knew the recipe could never be repeated, we declined all future summonses. Then Nikolaus became ill, and the dinners ceased.

28

The Companionship of Snooping

THE PLASH OF the stone in the pond making widening circles is a familiar simile to describe the extension of friendships, and how much I have enjoyed my own plash. In 1958 the Drawings Collection at the RIBA was given its own designated accommodation, on the fourth floor of 68 Portland Place. The kitchen there was a forerunner of the one that became so famous after we moved to 21 Portman Square, and helped to make the Collection a focus for the community of architectural historians. No other drawings collection could field such a team. After I succeeded Prunella Fraser as Curator in 1962, my assistants included Sandra Wedgwood, Sandra Milliken, Johanna Symonds and George McHardy, but the long-serving stalwarts were Jill Lever and Margaret Richardson. A bevy of brilliant young archi-tectural historians was brought in to catalogue drawings in their field of expertise and added to the camaraderie. When John McAndrew was working on his catalogue of Antonio Visentini drawings he wrote from the United States: 'Every day's an archi-tectural conference at Portman Square — and your lunches!' We were a well-spring of books and catalogues: in twenty-five years we produced more than thirty related to the contents of the Collection.

Some people called in to study specific drawings, some just because they were passing through London – my American friend Henry Russell Hitchcock, an annual visitor, always made a bee-line for the Collection to pick up all the latest gossip about who was working on what. By about 1963 we had become a sort of architectural hotbed of discussion. It needs to be stressed that in the early 1960s the RIBA's Drawings Collection was the first specialized archive to make architectural drawings available on an organized basis – tools for all – and also the first to put in place an acquisitions policy, one that has built the Collection from about 80,000 drawings to nearly half a million.

It was natural that the Collection should attract anyone who had anything to do with architectural history. The place fizzed with life as the architectural schools began to discover that here was ample material for student essays and projects. Michael Jaffe in Cambridge sent all his students – John Cornforth, Alan Tait, Alaistair Rowan, Marcus Binney, Gavin Stamp, David Watkin among the more distinguished few – as did Howard Colvin in Oxford – J. Mordaunt Crook and John Martin Robinson. So many friendships were initiated or matured in or through the Drawings Collection. Mark Girouard, one of my first friends in the business, could often be found there, working upon his doctoral thesis on Robert Symthson. Through Francis Watson I met Desmond Fitz-Gerald, Knight of Glin, known to us as Knighty, who in turn introduced me to the Irish Georgian Society and of course to Mariga and Desmond Guinness. What a contrast to our own staid and polite Georgian Group, at that time anxious never to be difficult – as when, in 1967, they sipped tea (it seemed) while the exquisite neo-classical Wilton Park in Buckinghamshire, a masterpiece exhibiting the combined talents

of Richard Jupp and C.H. Tatham, was replaced by a hideous
Ministry tower block. The Irish Georgians put them to shame,
battling royally and pulling no punches. They also made architectural history *fun*, not least through Mariga's wicked sense of
humour and willingness to visit country houses at all hours.

Then Gervase Jackson-Stops appeared at the Collection.
Martin Drury, his boss at the National Trust, said of him
recently: 'Not a day passes without his name and face crossing
my mind.' Gervase's was a short but phenomenal life. We were
discussing mortality, at some point before his revelation that he
was HIV positive. 'But Gerv,' I said, 'I'm not worried by death,
only the manner of it. After all, just think, you and I have led the
sort of rich lives denied to so many.' His eyes shone with pleasure.

He was constantly on the move, his work for the Trust requir-
ing him to criss-cross England. There was no barricade he could
not surmount. Once we arrived at Strensham church in
Worcestershire to see the Russell moments. The church door
was locked but the west aisle window was covered in scaffolding. Gervase was up it like a shot, prising open a window, and I
watched his little body disappear inside, head and hands first. Life
never allowed him the time to devote to a great book, but there
were brilliant articles, every one hand-written with a pen, and
always completed at the last possible moment. Eileen and I were
his laughing companions of passage, latterly in company with his
friend, the brilliant young gardener Ian Kirby. They were known
as House and Garden, 'House' for obvious reasons in Gervase's
case, 'Garden' because Ian had designed the garden at Gervase's
Menagerie at Horton in Northamptonshire. Ian was Eileen's
mentor too in gardening, so that gardens, and garden nurseries
in particular, became woven into many of our later forays; he followed Gervase as a casualty of Aids.

In 1972 Marcus Binney and I were asked by Roy Strong to curate what became the *Destruction of the Country House* exhibition held at the Victoria and Albert Museum in 1974. Marcus was then at *Country Life*, as were many bred in the hot-house of the Art History faculty at Cambridge. A by-product of the exhibition, which brought Marcus to the fore, was his foundation in 1975 of SAVE Britain's Heritage. A quarter of a century on, one can probably say that Marcus has done more than anyone to save our built environment. His quest led further, to the founding of SAVE Europe's Heritage, and to joint forays with him abroad: to Portugal many times from the late 1980s on, to record the lost gardens of the *quintas*; to Gibraltar for a report on the Rock's abuse of its heritage; to Jamaica in 1991 with Kit Martin to produce *Jamaica's Heritage: an untapped resource*; to what was then Czechoslovakia in 1994, to study their castles and country houses, in even worse crisis than our own.

In March 1995 I lured Tim Knox (by his friends familiarly known as Snake) out of the Drawings Collection to assist Gervase, who was by then growing very weak, at the Trust. There could have been no better choice to succeed my beloved friend as the Trust's Architectural Historian and, most recently, Chief Curator of Collections. Tim and his friend Todd Longstaffe-Gowan, whom I call The Tall One, in their turn became boon companions on our later snoops.

29

'Mr Adams lived in the village'

I T WAS 1965, and I was in the Print Room of the Metropolitan Museum in New York, quivering with excitement. I had already pulled out Sir William Chambers's designs for Kew Gardens, no less, and now I had in my hands an album of ceiling designs by James Wyatt, bought by the Museum in Paris as recently as 1958, an architectural treasure-trove documenting more than thirty-five houses by that notable claret-swiller. In particular it strengthened the evidence for his otherwise weakly documented Irish practice: Castlecoole, Curraghmore, Dungannon, Farnham, Slane, and a design for a certain 'Lord Knapton'. When I asked Desmond Fitz-Gerald about this man, Knighty immediately recognized 'Knapton' as a de Vesci title and exclaimed with loud hot passion, 'But that must be Abbeyleix! Belongs to Susan de Vesci. We must go there.' Howard Colvin's eyebrows rose at least an inch when he heard of this addition to Wyatt's *œuvre*.

We read in *Georgian Mansions in Ireland* (1915) that the sitting room at Abbeyleix contained 'Adam ornament' and a 'conventional Adam ceiling and frieze', but there are hints of difficulties encountered in the writer's comment that, 'owing to the absence of the owner at the Anglo-German war', access for photography had been denied. Desmond and I soon discovered that 'denial' was strongly characteristic of a family entrenched in the *status quo*. Of course, in view of my discovery in New York, there was no question of Robert Adam having designed Abbeyleix.

So with Desmond's friend Ann-Louise Stockdale and Eileen, we set forth to lunch with Viscountess de Vesci, who had informed Desmond that the Belgian Ambassador would also be present. We had been warned that Susan de Vesci, Lord Snowdon's sister, was not the brightest jewel in the crown. Our hearts thumped with excitement as we approached this undocumented house. The exterior was gloomy and dull, thanks to a stucco refacing about 1860 by T.H. Wyatt which had given it the look of a Late Classical Victorian house. From the moment we knocked on the door at midday everything went wrong. Lady de Vesci was frosty and sharp: 'I think you're wasting your time with this Weeart [*sic*], but come in,' she said, and then added, looking deliberately at her wrist-watch, 'Lunch is sharp at one.' In the company of this unbending chatelaine we perambulated the rooms in double-quick time. I produced my photographs of the Wyatt designs, matching ceiling with design, room by room. The Drawing Room had pretty William Morris wallpaper, reminding us that Evelyn de Vesci, whose husband had inherited Abbeyleix in 1875, three years after their marriage, had been one of The Souls. There was ample evidence that Lord Knapton (this was shortly before he was created Viscount de Vesci) had commissioned from Wyatt a new but plain house. As Desmond waxed enthusiastic about Wyatt in Ireland, Lady de Vesci looked stonily irritable. Behind her back Desmond made a face. The drink we were thirsting for never materialized, but when the bell went for lunch, there was the Belgian Ambassador, smiling, a large gin and tonic in his hand.

Although Knighty and I were flankers to Lady de Vesci, she trilled banalities across the table to the ambassador, entirely excluding us. Then, as she later confessed, Ann-Louise deliberately did for us. She had earned her doctorate with a study of William H. Sheppard, whose book *Presbyterian Pioneers in the Congo* (1916) had helped expose the murderous regime there of King Leopold. She piped up, 'Mr Ambassador, has your country come to terms with King Leopold's atrocities in the Congo?' Lady de Vesci blanched and dropped her dessert fork on her side plate. The ambassador's face was suffused with crimson, and he stuttered sharply, 'That is all now past history.' 'But that's not what's written in your school books, Mr Ambassador,' retorted Ann-Louise. 'They avoid the issue entirely.' Our hostess's complexion fluctuated between white and red through what seemed an interminable silence. Then it was suddenly all too much for her. Rising, she slapped her napkin down so hard that she sent her wine glass flying, and announced haughtily, 'It's time you left.' The ambassador still sat there, transfixed by Ann-Louise's accusations. As we were hustled towards the open front door, Lady de Vesci turned to Knighty. 'What nonsense about this Weeart, Mr Fitz-Gerald. He was never here. We have always known that Mr Adams lived in the village.' The door crashed shut behind us and we could no longer control our laughter. We could see our ex-hostess's white face at the window. She never spoke to Knighty again. The de Vescis are no longer in residence, and Abbeyleix has been beautifully restored by Sir David Davies, who declares himself an enthusiastic *aficionado* of 'Mr Weeart'.

30

The Chuckle House

Hazlewood

'KNIGHTY,' I SAID to Desmond Fitz-Gerald, Knight of Glin, one day in 1966, 'you've simply got to write that book about Richard Castle and the Palladian architecture of Ireland.' Castle, or Castles as he was sometimes named, was a leading Irish architect of the 1730s to 1760s, and the subject of Knighty's Harvard doctoral thesis. It was a book just *asking* to be published. He acquiesced in my bullying, and a tour of Castle's houses was put in train. Our party comprised Knighty, Eileen and myself.

Short of a helicopter to hop across the Shannon, we had to make a long loop from Glin Castle by way of Limerick to reach the north bank, Co. Sligo and Lough Gill, on the edge of which Castle had built Hazlewood in 1731 for Owen Wynne. Knighty was in great fettle. He had never been there, although he knew it from photographs: a main block linked by curved passages to advanced pavilions. 'Hope we can get in,' mused Knighty. 'It's a loony bin now. We call them Chuckle Houses.'

The weather was auspicious for visiting a lunatic asylum. Across the lough scudded gloomy rain clouds, from which the house seemed to emerge. It looked like so many Ascendency

19. The Chuckle House: Hazlewood, Co. Sligo (Irish Architectural Record)

mansions abandoned in the Troubles, its stonework black and stained, its drive unkempt, the park ploughed right up to the house, the windows so dirty they no longer reflected the light. There were no obvious signs of occupation, and as we approached we shivered a little. It was all rather disturbing.

As we jerked on a rusty bell-pull at the main door we admired the crisply-cut architectural centrepiece, the tripartite arrangement of door and side windows under the pedimented embrace of blocked attached columns. Above the pediment was a beautiful Ionic Palladian window, but with niches where outer windows might have been expected. A large grotesque mask seemed to be laughing at the plight of the chucklers within. This and the blank oculi above were Castle's decorative trademarks, his signature, used by him at Westport, too, also in Sligo. A faraway jangle had been audible when we pulled the bell, but no one came. We waited and pulled again. Still no one came. We shuffled. Then an unexpected shout caused us to do an about-turn, to be confronted by a man peering out of one of the pavilion's side doors. He was dressed in green linen overalls long since due for the laundry, and black curly hair hid his ears. 'I'm Mick, and wot d'yer want?' Knighty explained our mission. ''Tis a bad place we look after here, Mr Fitz-Gerald. Ill heads, you know. But come in.' Grimy passages, glossy cream and green paint, bare light-bulbs, stone-flagged floors, like a reformatory. We were ushered into an office: metal cabinets, pegs on the wall for more grubby green overalls, gas cooker with greasy saucepans, sink overflowing with dirty cups and saucers, the pattern of the lino floor obscured by ingrained dirt.

Mick returned with Eddie, whose left arm hung limp, his hand mangled, red and raw. We could not help but stare. Noticing, he explained equably: 'German tanks rolled over it at Beda Fomm.' He was introduced as a nursing assistant, the Keeper of the Keys, which were on a large ring held in his good fist. 'Now, don't worry,' said Mick reassuringly. 'The Chuckles, they're mostly harmless. Don't have to use this often,' indicating an electric-shock stick. ('But this is 1966!' The thought flashed through all our minds.) Eddie opened a large double door, surely once shining mahogany, now painted gloss green, leading into the Palladian hall. God, it was grand: massive Doric woodwork, the whole tied in by a heavy, finely carved Doric entablature. The panelled walls were punctuated by niches topped with swags. The original floor of black and white paving stones was there, but the white squares were themselves nearly black with dirt.

What Irish splendour! Castle would have had no trouble recognizing his creation – but not the unbelievable filth, in a band up to about five feet from the floor, rubbed there by bodies (and worse), streaked by the nervous scrapings of hundreds of fingernails. Six or seven Chuckles all dressed in coarse brown linen stood silent and mostly immobile at our entry. There was a stench of unwashed bodies. Wooden benches and a table comprised the furniture. One man was asleep in a corner, his head against the wall. Another stared, his eyelids covered with scabs. Yet another sat on a bench rubbing his thigh continuously. The thick linen was worn threadbare. 'He never stops, not even in his sleep. We must move on,' said Eddie. 'They get upset if they're being watched.' Mick pointed to a door, and said, 'Old staircase used to be here. They pulled it out in the Fifties. Was grand.' He opened the far door into, I think, the saloon. We passed through, and he locked it behind us. Here was a coved Palladian ceiling and plasterwork. Maybe ten brown-clad males, and more wooden benches. The same horrified recoil at sight of more greasy, nail-scraped walls. A fine grey stone Palladian chimney-piece had been broken through its pediment, and its opening reeked of urine. We were conscious of vacuous stares, just that. Mick nodded towards a man whose hands were incessantly 'knitting' – just the motion, no needles. 'He's knitted for eight years,' Mick said.

'Now for the women's ward, through this door. Take no notice of Annie, she's harmless.' Door unlocked, opened, closed, door locked. We were in the dining room, with access to the modern extension. Degraded decoration, from imperfect memory maybe early nineteenth-century. Knighty looked flushed. He was gazing fixedly at the saloon door behind him; perhaps he was trying not to think about what might happen if males got access to females. The women were dressed not in brown but in grey linen. Bare unstockinged legs, somewhat dirty, varicose veins. Strong body odours. Mostly elderly. But there was a *frisson* here, twitching faces, direct eye contact. Two women were talking incoherently to themselves, one straight into the corner of the room like a dunce. Another sat unmoving with her head in her hands. Suddenly, an ugly old crone moved towards us, laughing manically, and suddenly lifted her skirt to expose herself. Gave another shriek of laughter. Mick cautioned her away. It was a living enactment of a Hogarthian Bedlam.

Mick indicated it was time for us to leave, and as we passed through the garden entrance Knighty pointed out the Antique Roman style of the octagonal coffering of a vaulted ceiling: 'Pearce's influence!' he shouted – the innovative Irish Palladian architect Sir Edward Lovett Pearce had been Castle's master. Mick and Eddie let us out at the back. We had been hoping to explore the decayed garden laid out on the peninsula into the lough, to find the ruined grotto and the foundations of the Corinthian Temple to (of all gods, in view of the Chuckles) Aesculapius, but it was not to be. The rain simply lashed down and even as we turned to look back at it, the mist obscured Hazlewood. We shivered as we had upon arriving, and pretended we had heard manic laughter celebrating our departure.

31

Grubby monkey of a man

Paul Ganz

NEW YORK, 1959, at Columbia University, Rudolph Wittkower to his wife Margot: 'Simian-like man came to my lecture today. Very shabby.' The following week: 'Can't think who that grubby man is. A woman with him today. Very plain. Not well-off.' The third week, now more than a little irritated: 'Their name is Ganz. Want us to come for a drink. Not sure. Who are they?' 'They' were Paul and Ula Ganz.

Worn down by the constantly-repeated refrain 'Do come for a drink', Rudi caved in to the person he had come to refer to in his mind as his 'ape', commenting to Margot, 'Let's get it over and done with. At least they listen intently to my lectures.' Neither remarked upon the fact that the address they had been given was in the best part of Park Avenue.

As they entered the apartment block Rudi looked questioningly at Margot. The elegant decorum of the entrance hall, the solicitous hall porter, the luxurious elevator were unexpected. The door to the apartment opened to reveal Paul, truly a model of simian ugliness, dressed – as they later discovered he always was – in a shabby brown jacket, baggy crumpled grey trousers and unpolished brown shoes. Behind him stood Ula, soft and white of face, in a green-patterned frock – attire as invariable as Paul's, they also later learnt: he had bought a thousand yards of the fabric at a bankruptcy sale and insisted from then on that Ula should make her own frocks, to save money. At the moment of first crossing the threshold, however, the Wittkowers were transfixed not by their welcoming hosts but by the wonderland of Old Masters that hemmed them in. Canvases covered every inch of wall, were propped on chairs, stood against furniture, covered every window except in the kitchen, or hung on doors. Two of three bathrooms had been converted into picture stores. Name an Old Master and it seemed the Ganzes had at least one example of his work, whether it be Rubens, Vasari, Guercino, Pontormo, the Carracci, del Piombo, Giordano, Ricci . . . and so on, and so on. There were literally hundreds of canvases. Paul was the brother of Victor Ganz, the eminent collector of Picasso, and both enjoyed huge fortunes made from costume jewellery.

In contrast to Paul's coarse Brooklyn accent, Ula's quiet voice betrayed upper-class Minnesota origins. Paul's reaction to the glorious works in his collection was bizarrely conveyed in crudely explicit words and gestures – 'Look at that paint, don't yer want to jerk off in front of it?', and the baggy trousering around his crotch would quiver. In contrast to this vulgarity, Ula expressed herself with quiet certitude and a devastating connoisseurship. Rudi later maintained that in all the years he had been involved in art history he had never met anyone with a comparable photographic memory. Ula's mind was like a computer, calling up what she had seen on her travels, relating a picture on the walls of one museum to another in a church or a palace somewhere else with astonishing speed. She was always right.

This remarkable facility was demonstrated to Eileen and

myself on many occasions, most memorably at Burghley House. It would go something like this: 'Paul, look at this *Deposition*. Don't you remember, Paul? Rome in 1962. S. Pietro in Vincoli. By Pomarancio. First altar on the left.' And it was. In her 'Paul, look at this' voice she identified a dozen canvases. Lord Exeter had invited us to view the private rooms of Burghley House at Stamford in Lincolnshire. We were to meet in the Great Hall. At Lord Exeter's approach Paul suddenly stiffened, then quivered, and out of his mouth poured adoring invective: 'Fucking Jesus. God shit. You're my hero. Olympics, 1928.' (As Lord Burghley, the Marquess had won the gold medal in the 400m hurdles.) They practically embraced. Over tea Lord Exeter remarked that he had never met anyone like Paul Ganz, which was surely true. They got on famously.

The standard tour of the Park Avenue apartment was accompanied by tales of Paul's contests with dealers. 'They're all fucking crooks. If they don't bring out their wares I make their lives miserable.' And so he did. Day after day he would appear and verbally abuse them until, in despair, they brought out what they didn't really want to sell. 'They tell me they haven't got anything. Load of crap. I teach those shits a lesson. If I don't pay them for a year, I save on the interest from my investments.' And so the tour would continue. As Eileen and I discovered for ourselves, it could last five hours. There was no escape. Paul would regale us with stories about his nocturnal wanderings up and down Park Avenue looking into the trash bins, and his many encounters. A favourite anecdote was how he got off jury duty by dressing in drag, complete with high heels and full make-up. 'Told them I hated niggers and gays. They told me to go, and never return.' Each picture demanded a discourse, usually an account of how he had successfully pitted his wits against the dealer who sold it to him. Then followed dinner, with the pleasure of a proper window to the outside world at last. Like Ula's dresses, the menu was unchanging: always chicken in a white sauce, green beans, apple pie and ice-cream. The wine was generally undrinkable. Once when we were there, Paul explained how he had demonstrated the male anatomy to his two lovely adopted daughters by dropping his own trousers.

You had to be a masochist to travel with Paul and Ula, but Eileen and I did so, many times. Although it was the last time, a week in Munich was typical. Ordered to book into the Bayerischer Hof on Promenadeplatz, we discovered that the Ganzes had a deal for a twenty-five per cent reduction for staying there every time they were in Munich. Dinner at a mediocre restaurant serving heavy German food involved another deal, a twenty per cent reduction for eating there every one of the six nights of our stay. Of course we had to comply. Paul's reaction to the everyday and commonplace was that of a child. He drove us insane. Every few minutes, as his eye lit upon something banal, came the rasping shout, 'Look at that cloud, Ula! Ula, there's a brown dog. Ula, there's a fountain.' Tony Clark told us that when he drove with them once from Rome to Naples, he wore ear-plugs.

On this particular Munich trip, I think Eileen and I both had a sense that it was time for our relationship with the Ganzes to end. We were irritated by having to visit the same dealer no fewer than five times. Four times there would be shrugs, gestures to the paintings on the walls, none of them of interest to Paul. But this was his wearing-down process: on the fifth visit, he triumphed, and out of store came a rare Januarius Zick. It was all very well for Paul and Ula, but we were screaming to get away to better things. Day six was an umbrella day, grey and wet. Lacking any small change for the Altes Pinakotek cloakroom, we asked Paul to pay the trivial charge. As we ascended those long stairs to the upper galleries we found we were no longer looking forward to his raucous responses to what he saw. Of an early gold-ground panel that had been over-zealously restored it was, 'Shit, Ula, look at this panel: fucking ruined'; of a mouth-watering Giordano, 'Jesus, Ula, makes me want to masturbate.' Had he done so, we would not have been surprised.

After we had left the museum Paul suddenly announced that he wanted to go to the British European Airways office, near the hotel. At the counter he pulled out a wodge of air tickets and asked for a flight to Milan. Eileen and I exchanged puzzled looks. We were all booked to return to London the next day. The girl pored over the schedules, did some arithmetic, and told Paul that to alter his original bargain-break ticket would involve an extra payment. At this Paul's face became suffused with red and out of his mouth poured a stream of such filth that we wished the earth might open up and swallow, if not him, then us. The receptionist called the manager, and the manager threatened to call the police. Eileen and I had had enough. We walked out, leaving Ula standing there in calm unconcern, as if such a tirade was a daily happening – as indeed it was. What pleasure we had that evening. Denied our sixth ghastly dinner, we celebrated in the best restaurant in Munich. We never saw Paul and Ula again. A few weeks later a letter from Paul in New York accused us in obscene language of criminal intent in not paying back the loan of the cloakroom fee.

Paul's ending was in character, and caused merriment all round. He and Ula, unable to contemplate life apart, had agreed a suicide pact: should one or the other become terminally ill, they would sit on the sofa together, hold hands, and swallow poison. Paul obtained the pills. Ula became ill, apparently without hope of recovery. It was the end. They popped their pills. Paul died immediately; Ula survived, and lived happily ever after.

32

Atishoo!

IN 1984 I was asked to contribute a paper on Inigo Jones and Elias Holl to a conference in Augsburg dedicated to Holl, the town's famous renaissance architect, who was not only a contemporary of Jones but like him looked to the Venetian architecture of Andrea Palladio for inspiration. In the accepted pedantic German academic tradition I was asked to send in my completed paper three months before the conference, so that it could be abstracted and delivered to selected respondents, enabling them to consider what I had to say and prepare a reasoned critical response, to be delivered publicly at the conclusion of my lecture. Among other matters, I had to consider whether Holl had designed the Englischebau at Heidelberg Castle. Presenting, towards the castle, the earliest Palladian façade in Germany, the new wing had been built for Frederick, the Elector Palatine, and his new wife Princess Elizabeth (later familiarly known as The Winter Queen), eldest daughter of James I of England. Inigo Jones enters the story because in 1613 he was one of the wedding party that accompanied Frederick and Elizabeth on their leisurely journey from London to Heidelberg.

As they travelled the Englischebau was building for their reception. I wrote my paper, basing it upon published literature and photographs of the castle, not least on what Henry Russell Hitchcock had had to say in his *German Renaissance Architecture* (1981), and sent it in as requested.

I must now confess to something awful. One cold winter's afternoon in 1964 Eileen and I made an excursion from Munich to Augsburg with Paul and Ula Ganz to see the Sigismund Röhrer collection of baroque and rococo oil sketches in the Schaezler-Palais. I had a streaming cold and had been sneezing all morning. In front of Maulpertsch's *St Martinus* my nose suddenly started to twitch, and an unstoppable sneeze shot a huge bogey out of my nose, just like a bullet, to land with a plop near the saint's right hand. I stared, horrified: it was obvious, and nasty. What could I do? If I attempted to wipe it off with a hanky, the alarms might ring; nor could I face the thought of confessing to a curator, in my stumbling German, that I had disfigured a work of art with a bogey. I concluded that I must quickly pass on.

I had visited Heidelberg Castle several times, but like most other visitors had never been able to make a proper physical examination of the Englischebau: its interior had been closed to the public ever since it was ruined in the late seventeenth century, and the north front clung precipitously to the cliff above the Rhine. On our way to the conference Eileen and I stopped in Heidelberg, and this time by sheer chance we met the Surveyor of the Castle. He was a great enthusiast, and methodically showed us all over the ruins of the Englischebau. Together we concluded that its building history must be completely rewritten. So must my lecture. While it was not possible to say with certainty that Inigo Jones had himself designed the Palladian elevation, it was possible to demonstrate that the change of style between the surprisingly full baroque of the north front and the Palladian of the south was made at the time when Jones was staying in the castle, perhaps supervising a masque in celebration of the Elector's nuptials.

When I informed my Augsburg audience that I had rewritten my lecture as a result of my serendipitous encounter at Heidelberg, it nearly caused a riot. There was a ripple of exclamation, as if such a proceeding were quite unprecedented. The respondents, so cleverly chosen for maximum effect, were left in confusion, as was the Chairman, who at the conclusion of my talk said, 'Mr Harris has taught us to look at the building.'

Eileen and I were not adept in the German language, so one morning we absented ourselves from the conference and revisited that delectable Röhrer Collection. As might be guessed, I made straight for the Maulpertsch of painful memory: the bogey was still there, now solidified. In 1996 I told this disgusting tale to James Miller, soon to be in Augsburg on Sotheby's business. On his return he confirmed my fears: it was *still* there, but now desiccated to a mere nasal blip in the surface varnish.

33

No winkies here

Bob Jones University

'B E OUR GUESTS,' wrote Bob Jones II, in response to our request in 1967 to see the Bob Jones University's famous gallery of religious art. We had an introduction from Julius Weitzner, who had sold most of the pictures to Bob Jones I and II. He had already told us, with some amusement, that a precondition of purchase was that all Divine winkies be covered with painted-on slips of cloth, to avoid over-stimulating the Christian Fundamentalist students.

From Charleston in South Carolina our Greyhound bus took us northwards along rural roads, roaring through many a poor township, as it passed enveloping dolorous people rocking away their lives on their verandas in hot, dry dust. We arrived in Greenville, North Carolina a day early. The next day we were expected to stay in the University, but for this night we found ourselves a comfortable motel opposite the university gates, little realizing the contrast between life outside the gates and life within. That evening we dined on juicy steaks and baked potatoes with mountains of butter and sour cream.

At ten next morning we presented ourselves at Bob Jones's office. He was not there, but we were warmly welcomed, and provided with Ellen, a poor-white girl from the Deep South Bible Belt, to conduct us to our accommodation and be our guide. Ellen seemed servile, too docile, and far too eager to please. We expected a room in a dormitory block, but were led to a freestanding shed, painted dark green and with no obvious windows apart from narrow horizontal lights high up on the wall. It was a room from which we could not look out and, naturally, those outside could not look in. This puzzled us, until we remembered Weitzner's advice to always bear in mind that this was a Christian Fundamentalist university. Quite clearly, we were 'forbidden fruit'. There were 'No Smoking' signs, and a library of Christian Fundamentalist books written by the Bob Joneses. As Ellen closed the door we burst out laughing. Should we leave rude graffiti, or perhaps a condom? At that time Eileen smoked a packet of cigarettes a day: she deliberately pulled one out and puffed away.

We had been instructed to have a look at the Art Gallery and then meet Ellen at the 'top of the slope' to the dining hall. The collection was astonishing, with splendid baroque works of art, including a rare de La Tour. The two Bobs had impeccable taste, but their patronage of expensive and important religious art seemed to us to sit uneasily in a university dedicated to imbuing poor southern whites with the sort of Christian teaching that narrows the arteries of both mind and soul.

Two hours passed quickly among such pictures, and it was time for lunch. We found Ellen standing just apart from a crowd of students milling around the entrance to what looked like a huge aircraft hangar – also painted green. All the students were white, of course, as Aryan as any regiment of Hitler Youth. We wondered what everyone was waiting for. Suddenly there was a crash of cymbals from a hi-fi amplifier. All eyes were raised to an elevated balcony and doorway, out of which stepped a priest dressed in black. His arms were raised, the Word of God was spoken, the massed congregation knelt in supplication, then rose and, to the sound of 'Onward! Christian Soldiers', marched on to lunch, not war. It was pure Cecil B. de Mille. We could hardly suppress our amusement.

The vast hangar-like hall must have held five hundred. All were standing, twelve to each table, arranged boy, girl, boy, girl, with an invigilator at each end. From an inside balcony a girl prefect offered up a grace, and we all sat down. The food was worse than my first meal in the army on basic training: watery hominy grits with something floating in them, followed by white boiled fish, and a gelatinous tapioca. We picked at the food and moved it around our plates. Barely had half an hour passed when from the tannoy sounded loud trumpets. It was a call to stand up again and give thanks to God for what Bob Jones had offered, whether people had finished or not. Everyone moved out in regimented order and so did we, closely guarded by Ellen. We were astonished to see the males automatically peel away from the females as they emerged from the shed. We learned that the sexes were segregated at all times, except at meals and in the evenings in a common room-cum-coffee shop.

Our Ellen then invited us to see the theatre workshop. Bob Jones II, an actor of some distinction, had a passion for amateur theatricals. To satisfy it he had bought the entire collection of costumes and stage effects of a major New York theatre when it closed down. The Bob Jones Theater would not have shamed the largest university in the USA. Attached to it was the university's own radio station, and a full-scale film studio. 'You are going to see excerpts from our latest film,' said the docile Ellen. We goggled in disbelief over a film about the American Civil

War, *The Blue and the Gray*, in which the Confederate Gray South won!

By late afternoon, Ellen was happy enough to leave us to our own devices. Perhaps she thought we needed some time to ourselves; she cannot have suspected the plans maturing in our minds. We indicated we would spend the evening in the library, and politely apologized for missing dinner. 'I'll collect you for breakfast,' she said, and bade us good-night. Our intention was to pack our bags, await darkness, and make a run for the freedom and luxury of the motel beyond the gates. In the library the reading room was full. We noticed that the newspaper rack held only selected, southern papers. The available journals had also clearly been carefully chosen. I did wonder whether the winkies had been painted out in these, too – and what about nipples? – but could find no evidence that they had been censored. I sat down, as did Eileen, elsewhere in the room. Glancing around, I felt as if something were wrong, the sort of feeling you get prior to discovering that you've been walking about with flies unzipped. I sensed a *frisson* of tension around me. Then it dawned: the library was segregated, and I was sitting among the girls! I had had enough of this bizarre place. Rising, I whispered to Eileen, 'Let's get out of here, p.d.q.' We collected our bags. The dark had settled in. Nervously we skirted the administrative offices, then ran helter-skelter out of that gate. As we did so I remembered Siegfried Sassoon's lines from 'Everyone Sang' and was 'filled with such delight As prisoned birds must find in freedom'.

Years later we told this tale to the distinguished Rubens scholar Julius Held, Eileen's old tutor at Barnard College. He too had once been invited by Bob Jones to the University, to lecture on Rubens with special reference to those of his works held in the gallery. Afterwards, he received public thanks, and an envelope containing the fee for his lecture. To the consternation of those present, and of Bob Jones II, Julius announced that he proposed to donate the money to the Civil Rights Movement.

34

Gangsters at Oak Spring

THE MELLON ESTATE in Virginia has been compared to an Arcadia out of one of the exquisite eighteenth-century hunting pictures Paul Mellon collected so enthusiastically. When the Brick House was built as the centrepiece of the estate in 1940, war had not yet come to America. Paul and Mary (Conover) Mellon were wealthy Americans of conventional taste, and it was only after Mary's sudden death in 1941 that Paul sought solace in Jung's psychiatry and grew in stature as a collector. The Brick House was a mirror of his Anglo-American Colonial-style taste. It was virtually a copy by the architect William Adams Delano of the celebrated eighteenth-century Hammond Harwood House in Annapolis, though in its time the Brick House could never have been confused with the real thing. After Paul married Rachel Lambert, always known as Bunny, in 1948, the house increasingly served as a museum facility for his British pictures, his library of sporting books and topography, the Degas waxes, and his curatorial staff. It was a place he often escaped to from his new house at nearby Oak Spring; I suspect he preferred it.

Oak Spring was built for Bunny, out of sight but just over the hill. Designed by the architect Page Cross, it was a house of a strikingly different sort, asymmetrical and loose-limbed in plan, and low, like a grand bungalow. Its interior, featuring Bunny's sympathetic, Provençal taste in colours, fabrics and furniture, laced with mementoes and references to her gardening skills, was no showcase for dull British Georgian pictures, but rather for her preferred Impressionist and Post-Impressionist paintings, some of the greatest ever painted. If the Brick House was masculine in an American gentleman's club style, Oak Spring was a joyfully feminine place.

As a consultant on Paul's London Advisory Board I used to visit Mellonville, and when I did so I might be accommodated either in the Brick House or at Oak Spring. I preferred the Brick House for its agreeable housekeeper who provided sustaining breakfasts, and for the possibility it offered of informal behaviour. I have two particular recollections of staying with the Mellons, once in the Brick House, once at Oak Spring.

The perimeters of the Mellon estate are protected as if by a *cordon sanitaire*. Once a visitor has passed from public road to private drive, discreet cameras follow his progress, monitored from a security room and with security services backed up by emergency and reserve systems. No stranger could possibly just drive in for a 'hit and run'. This was necessary for a man of Mellon's wealth, but none the less it was a source of myth and legend, especially with regard to Oak Spring: Willis van Devanter, Paul's librarian, used to giggle that it was better to stay in the Brick House, because at Oak Spring there were secret cameras to observe every indiscretion in the bedrooms.

The Brick House was more environmentally controlled than any other house I know, and almost any museum. The air conditioning was so discreet as to seem non-existent. Of course, windows could not be opened; after all, that might damage the paintings. One evening, having retired to bed, I was brought out of it again near midnight by the breathless arrival of Willis, who lived in a cottage on the estate. He was distraught. Disaster loomed. The air-conditioning had broken down, and so had the back-up plant. Paul had been informed, and had sent his jet to collect Carter Brown, Director of the National Gallery of Art in Washington, for an urgent consultation. I was very slow. 'Why the panic?' I asked. 'There's NO AIR-CONDITIONING,' Willis reiterated, looking at me strangely. Could I not understand? Books, drawings, Degas waxes, paintings – all were in jeopardy.

The scream of a jet could be heard as Carter arrived at the private airfield with a posse of National Gallery conservationists, all of whom had no doubt been hauled from their beds. I stood apart, goggling over the earnest discussions about summoning air-conditioned vans to remove everything to Washington, as if every object in the house needed life support. There were frantic calls to various organizations, and for all I know many more beds were emptied. Air-conditioning engineers were on their way with a police escort.

It was now about two-thirty in the morning, and it was a circus. I was greatly amused. The books had survived in country-house libraries without the least vestige of 'environmental protection' since being printed. The early paper of the drawings was quite able to stand up to most fluctuations in temperature. Before their discovery and purchase by Paul Mellon, the Degas waxes had been stored in a cellar for thirty years. As for the paintings, what had been the conditions inside the country houses whose walls they had once adorned, especially in winter? 'It's all barmy,' I said to Willis, causing his chin and eyes to flutter rather more than usual. The engineers arrived at four, and by five the controls were back in place. The cost must have been phenomenal.

Then at breakfast the housekeeper said to Willis: 'But Mr van Devanter, don't you remember when the air-conditioning broke down in 1970? Old Mr Jenny in Middleburg just came over and mended it.' Willis went very pink. Yet, he would agree, it was all barmy.

Perhaps this is the moment to relate the sad tale of my old friend Willis. I met him in the early 1960s when I was invited by Paul Mellon to advise him on making a collection of English architectural books. As a library graduate at Yale, Willis had been befriended by Jim Babb, Yale Librarian and an alumnus of Paul's class. 'I need a young assistant to help with my books,' said Paul to Babb, and got Willis. Neither Babb nor Yale foresaw the consequences: within a few months, Willis van Devanter had become the most powerful book buyer in America. The stuffy academics at Yale were Not Amused, and there ensued a policy of withering denigration of Willis's efforts and reputation. The pedants were determined to wreak their revenge. Yet Willis was himself one of Paul's most remarkable acquisitions. He was a perfect bookman and had great taste. If he lacked the stamina for the physical work of cataloguing books, he was full of enthusiasm and possessed of a most catholic knowledge. In his financial dealings he behaved impeccably, with the utmost honesty and probity. Had he so wished, he could have been a very rich man, for booksellers were clamouring to shower him with pecuniary inducements. He took not a cent.

The richness of Paul's printed sporting and topographical collections and the extraordinary growth of his collection in other related subjects owed everything to Willis. Once Paul Mellon had bought Major Abbey's great library of topographical books – now recognized to have been one of his greatest acquisitions – Willis was the inspiration and motivator for its enlargement.

Yale refused to contemplate any involvement by Willis in what subsequently became the Yale Center for British Art, yet as Willis wrote to me, 'I don't want to be Rare Book Librarian. I am rather a back-room boy.' On my last visit to Upperville I was much struck by his unhappiness. Neither Paul nor Yale would tell him what his future would be. The uncertainty fed all his neuroses, and led to his sudden departure from the Brick House. In the course of what I think was probably my last conversation with Paul Mellon I raised the matter of Willis's future. Confrontational as ever, I extolled him and his virtues. All I got was a tightening of the mouth and the comment, 'It's up to Yale.' As I discovered later, I too was in disgrace (see chapter 35). Paul was never one to tackle problems head-on.

Yale's final assault on Willis's reputation can be found in the Acknowledgements in the Mellon catalogue *Books on the Horse and Horsemanship*, by John B. Podeschi (1981). Even eight years after Willis's dismissal – he who had been instrumental in forming the collection – his name does not appear: only that of Mary Ann Thompson, described by Podeschi as 'Keeper of Mr Mellon's books', whatever that may mean. Rumours were rife among bookmen that Podeschi's first draft for the Acknowledgements had been sanitized by Yale, and I can readily believe it.

Evenings at Oak Spring always began pleasantly and traditionally with Paul's ritual bullshots, which he mixed to perfection, followed by dinner, always notable for the French cuisine and vintage wines and the pleasure of being able to look, as one ate, at one of the greatest of Van Gogh's flower paintings. The habit of retiring early also pleased me.

The particular Oak Spring evening I recall, Paul introduced me to the writings of Frederick Prokosch, notably his poetry.

Shortly after we had all gone to bed, I went down again to borrow Prokosch's *Carnival*. It was very stormy outside. Alone in the book room, I began to wonder where the hidden camera was, and as a tease put out my tongue. Back upstairs I was soon warmly tucked up in bed reading what became one of my favourite poems – 'Pears on the boughs hung golden, the street lay still and cool, children with books and satchels, came sauntering home from school' – before falling asleep.

I awoke feeling chilly, as if the gentle heating had been turned off, and indeed it had. Having dozed off without benefit of a last toilet break, I needed the bathroom. I reached out to one bedside lamp, but nothing happened. Out went my arm to the other – still no light. Odd, I thought, and got up to try the wall light. Still nothing. A power failure, I wondered? Having peed in the dark, I left the bathroom and lifted the telephone. It too was dead.

I stood pondering, staring out of the window into blackness. The storm had abated. From my window I had a view of the entrance forecourt and directly ahead, up the drive, to the rise of the hill towards the Brick House beyond the summit, and the exit roads. At first all was dark, then the trees were suffused with the light of two approaching cars. They drew up, and out sprang three men, one holding a gun! So this was it: Paul was to be kidnapped, and all communication with the outside world had been cut. My watch said half-past three. What should I do?

I remembered that Father Robert Casey, Chaplain and Dean of Sidney Sussex College, Cambridge, who was on the ill-fated *Lusitania* when she was torpedoed, had commented later that, as far as he was concerned, it was 'everyone for themselves'. In this present critical situation there seemed to be no place for heroics on my part. What better place to hide than in a tiny box-room I had discovered under the eaves, behind a low door in the bathroom. I collected two pillows, crawled in, and hid behind a large suitcase with which I blocked the door. 'Now we'll know how Mellon values himself,' I thought, speculating upon the likely size of the ransom.

In discomfort I waited maybe an hour, until suddenly a gleam of light appeared around the door. I froze, but it was accompanied by no sound of approaching gangsters looting the house. After a hushed moment of suspense I gently opened the door, to find all the lights on. The telephone was working again, and there was no car in the entrance drive. My watch said half-past five. I lay in bed for a while, then decided to get dressed, and went nonchalantly down to replace *Carnival* on the library shelves. The sudden appearance of a maid startled me – she also seemed startled, obviously unused to encountering guests at dawn. She said, 'Good morning, sir. I hope you were not inconvenienced by the big power cut last night. Storm blew up and a tree fell across the telephone line. The back-up systems all blew. Hope the security men did not disturb you.'

I blushed, thought of Father Casey with his genuine dilemma of conscience, and returned to the traditional Oak Spring breakfast in bed. Remembering Willis van Devanter's giggles about security cameras in the bedrooms, I examined my room with care to see if I could spot where they were, and work out whether my cowardly antics were now the butt of hilarity in the basement security room.

35

The Cox–Turner débâcle

I<small>T MUST HAVE</small> been in the 1960s that I received a book catalogue from the antiquarian booksellers, Sawyer's. One item
immediately took my notice: a *History of the Manor of Marden*, by
Lord Coningsby. The catalogue described it as a guide to
Hampton Court in Herefordshire, in black-letter Latin, printed
privately in the 1720s. Bound in with it were some topographical engravings and two water-colour views of Hampton Court
attributed to David Cox. A price of £80 persuaded me to add
it to my collection of country-house guides.

Disappointment when it arrived: the handsome red calf
binding with an unrecognizable gilt coat of arms opened only
on a boring demonstration by Lord Coningsby of his claim to
the barony of Marden in Herefordshire. Family history and
genealogy were passions of this lord, obsessed as he was with his
lineage. It was not a history of his seat. I contemplated returning it to Sawyer's, but Leonard Knyff's engraved view of
Hampton Court and the attractive water-colours persuaded me
to put the quarto on my shelves for a while.

Time passed, and Paul Grinke, friend and antiquarian bookseller, came to dinner. I showed him Coningsby's volume. He looked at it gloomily and commented deprecatingly that it would be 'not easy to sell' – but then recognized the coat of arms as being that of Colt Hoare of Stourhead, and agreed to put it in a catalogue. What did I want for it? 'Only my costs,' I replied, suggesting he take it to Dudley Snelgrove for his opinion as to whether the water-colour views were by Cox. Dudley was an authority on English water-colours and, with Judy Egerton, was in charge of Paul Mellon's London office in Dover Street, where all the invoices for Mellon's book and drawing acquisitions were processed and the acquisitions themselves prepared for shipment. I was at that time the architectural book advisor responsible to Mellon's Librarian, Willis van Devanter, and ultimately to Mellon himself.

Time again passed, at least a couple of years I think, and I had completely forgotten the Marden volume until one night, sitting in bed with Kenneth Woodbridge's new book on Stourhead, *Landscape and Antiquity* (1970), I received a shock: here was a letter from Sir Richard Colt Hoare, requesting J.M.W. Turner, when he was next in Herefordshire, to 'make two views of Hampton Court for my Marden'. But where was the *Marden* I had bought? Although it was past midnight I rang Paul Grinke. He grumbled sleepily that he'd look in the morning, to which I retorted that I hoped he had it because I had certainly not been paid my eighty pounds! What a sleepless night that was for me.

Next morning Paul rang back, mystified. He didn't have it, but had never put it in a catalogue, and could find no invoice. 'But what about Dudley Snelgrove?' I asked. Paul then recollected that he had taken the volume to the Dover Street office: Dudley was not there, only a female secretary, to whom Paul gave the message asking for Dudley's opinion as to whether the water-colours in the book were by Cox. As with me, it had then

20. Hampton Court, Herefordshire, J.M.W. Turner, *c.* 1795

slipped his mind completely. With all speed I hastened to Dover Street, and there lying flat and forgotten on a lower shelf was the *Marden*, its red calf binding covered in dust. As it was of course still mine I took the volume, and told the secretary I had done so. The possible repercussions of this action never occurred to me.

I had the water-colours taken out of the volume and framed, and eventually the book itself was sold at Sotheby's along with other selections from my library. The Turners hung at home until I was persuaded to put them into a selling exhibition of English water-colours at Colnaghi's. 'They'll be a cert. for Mellon,' I was told, but after the exhibition they were returned to me unsold. Dudley had apparently paused in front of them, and passed on without comment.

On 27 June 1972 the great sale at Hampton Court in Herefordshire took place. It was the sort of country-house sale that today we look back on with envy. The stars were the two oil landscape views of the house painted by Leonard Knyff in 1699. Bill Drummond of Sidney Sabin was commissioned by Mellon to purchase one for £20,000, and the other was bought for stock for £23,000. Around these in 1973 Bill Drummond formed an exhibition entitled *A Country House Portrayed: Hampton Court, Herefordshire* which also included my Turners, a late seventeenth-century water-colour survey of Hampton Court, the Knyff engravings, and a portrait of Lord Coningsby by the Irish painter Thomas Bate, bought from the same sale by Sabin for Mellon but stopped for export on behalf of the Belfast Museum. When he was next in London Mellon bought the other Knyff as well, and my Turners. Today they are in the Yale Center for British Art.

So ended the story that began with a book from Sawyer's and a letter from Colt Hoare to Turner. It left my reputation in tatters, and it was a while before I was able to work out why. The Colnaghi dealer put me on the scent and then I faxed my friend Judy Egerton, who confessed that until the day of Dudley Snelgrove's death he believed the water-colours to have been stolen from Mellon, and she did too. It seems not to have occurred to them that a book bought on Mellon's behalf must necessarily have an invoice to match it, and this of course did not exist. Since the book had not been sold to Mellon I had not stolen it – but the general view that I *had* explained a number of things: the injudicious comment made by a member of the Yale Center's staff, to the effect that as far as Mellon was concerned I was 'a hot potato'; Mellon's reluctance to finance the previously promised last year of my consultancy contract after the Yale Center opened in 1974; and his icy coldness to me when I was Mellon Lecturer in Washington in 1982.

36

Not Karlskoga

WHENEVER I TRAVELLED on the Continent for business reasons I tried to add a day to my schedule, a day dedicated to my own pleasures. In a capital or other large city the routine was to arrive at the railway station, examine possible destinations and departure times, and leave on a train within thirty minutes. The maximum travelling time must be no more than about two hours each way, so as to allow me perhaps six to eight hours to enjoy my destination. All choices must be made within that half-hour (and no more): there must be no pre-planning – it must a *journée de surprise*. No day was ever such a surprise as the one that began in a train I took from Stockholm one early winter's morning in 1978.

The board announced a train for Malmö connecting to Karlskrona, due to depart in twenty minutes at eight o'clock. I'd heard of Karlskrona – was it not Sweden's great naval base? But where was it? I glanced at a small-scale map in my guidebook, and there it was, roughly due west of Stockholm, near Lake Vänern, just inland from Kristinehamn. That would do: it looked like a trip of about an hour and a half. Naval base? It must be an inland one, with a canal exit to the sea. I hurriedly bought a ticket, so hurriedly that in my impatience I neither converted the cost out of kronor, nor queried the booking clerk's surprise that I was planning to return that day. He said something about 'Alvesta' that also escaped me.

What a fine train, so sleek and modishly modern, and so comfortable. I collapsed with pleasure into an embracing seat, ready to enjoy speeding through wintry snow forests in sybaritic warmth. Departure was imminent, and the announcement in Swedish did not alert me to the significance of Malmö. But the cost of the ticket in kronor nagged at me: had I been overcharged? Only now did I do my arithmetic, and the conversion produced a fare of £110. I was horrified. This was far too much for my estimated distance of only about ninety miles. There was nothing I could do, however, and as the train pulled out I squinted at the map again. With consternation I realised it was Karlskoga, not Karlskrona, that was ninety miles west of Stockholm. I sagged in my seat. Where was Karlskrona?

When the train drew in to Linköping it was clear to me that I was going not west but south, and as confirmation there was Karlskrona on my map, on the Baltic on the very south-east corner of Sweden. When the ticket inspector arrived I decided to keep mum. 'Change at Alvesta,' he said, and upon my asking when, replied, 'three-fifty, and an hour to wait. You arrive at Karlskrona an hour and a half later.' I resigned myself to my fate. Miles of monotonous snowy forests sped by, but coffee came round, and an agreeable lunch whiled away the hours until Alvesta. It was little more than a junction. I walked a street of dull shops and found one selling creamy buns and hot coffee.

So at six I was in Karlskrona, and it was too dark for any detailed examination. Exiting from the station I encountered late nineteenth-century façades and, on busy Ronnebygatan, a hotel.

A brochure at the desk informed me that this part of the town had been razed by fire in 1887 and that Karlskrona was the old island of Trosso, chosen by Charles IX in 1680 when he decided to move his country's naval headquarters from the Swedish Archipelago to the more southerly ice-free waters of the Baltic. I would look for a restaurant and, more importantly, a toothbrush and razor. As I wandered about I began to notice the evidence of grand, formal urban planning, the streets laid out on a grid pattern. I entered an oblong *place*, to be suddenly transported to baroque Rome, no less. Here was Stortorget, with churches and buildings as Roman as could be. Both the Fredriks church, based upon S. Trinita dei Monti, and the Trinity church dated from the 1680s. All the signs and street language were maritime and military: *Fortificat gatan, Amiralitets gatan, Vall gatan.* From the brochure I had learned that this was a new town, like Louis XIV's Rochfort, and that architecturally the design had been shared by the Swedish architect and Director-General of Fortifications Count Erik Dahlbergh and Nicodemus Tessin the younger, both of whom had stamped it with their experiences of the Rome of Sixtus V and Louis XIV's Paris. I was able to identify what I was now seeing with the Tessin style that is such a characteristic of Caroline Stockholm. My spirits rose. By mistaking Karlskoga for Karlskrona I had given myself much to discover.

I rose early and walked through the leafy Admiralty Garden bisected by the narrow-gauge naval railway that served the dockyards. I found the Admiralty church, again thoroughly Roman in a Tessin style, but by Dahlbergh in 1685, and paused in front of the neo-classic Naval Yard Guardhouse (1819), colourwashed in that typical Swedish yellow-ochre. What was beyond the Admiralty security gates I could not fathom. But I began with breakfast in the fish market, then became the first visitor of the day at the Blekinge County Museum, housed the palace built by either Dahlbergh or Tessin in 1703 for Count Hans Wachmeister, original instigator of the naval move here.

The Marine Museum was an obvious port of call. It would tell me much about the development of the dockyard, which I was now impatient to see, having remembered that Sir William Chambers was a friend of Vice-Admiral Fredrik Hendrik af Chapman, the great ship designer, also reputed to be something of an architect. He had subscribed in 1759 to Chambers's *Treatise on Civil Architecture*, and Chambers had supervised the London distribution of his great work on naval architecture, the *Architectura navalis mercatoria* (1768). But in any case, maritime museums are always repositories of fascinating and unexpected works of art.

I found not only the unexpected but also Svante Warfvinge, an enthusiastic young man who was the historian of the dock-yard buildings designed by af Chapman. For Svante – and for me in his wake – the gates of the Guard House opened, as did the Admiralty church, the Wood Carver's Workshop designed by af Chapman in 1784, many neo-classical Gustavian buildings, and the amazing Great Rope Yard of 1691, reputedly the longest building in Sweden. But the greatest treasure Svante opened with his magical key – and a telephone call to the current Count Wachmeister in Stockholm – was not in the Yards, but at Skärva, af Chapman's own house, built in the 1780s on a rocky wooded headland across the water.

Descriptive words fail me. It was marooned in a sea of ice, and I prostrated myself on an icy path and smashed my camera, but Skärva was the house I coveted most in the world – and I still do. It is the bungalow to out-bungalow all others, and so chic. Roofed as it originally was in turf, it was the epitome of a barge-boarded, Nashesque, Reptonesque, Picturesque *cottage orné*. Af

21. C.A. Ehrensvärd's Greek portico at Skärva, Karlskrona,
Sweden

Chapman sketched out its informal plan, with its magical tent-
like octagonal rotunda, and his ship-builders and woodcarvers
brought it to life. A little later Carl August Ehrensvard of Greek
Revival fame added the noble Paestum Doric portico. Inside
there remained many furnishings that af Chapman would recognize, even his drawing office, outside were the surrounding
dark trees, the icy-blue glint of the sea, the garden ornamental-
ized in Chambers's Kew manner with temples and hermitages,
and a gothic monument copied from Thomas Carter's engravings in his *Builder's Magazine*. I paid icy homage at af Chapman's
melancholy Druidic rock tomb in a grove of trees, looking across
to his beloved dockyards. All conspired to enchant.

37

The unburdening

Osaka

I N 1966 I was asked to contribute a section on the architecture of Inigo Jones to a British Council exhibition commemorating Britain's first trade mission to Japan. What nonsense, I thought. It was to be staged in, of all unsuitable places, a Mitsukoshi department store in Osaka, and then in another in Tokyo. The Mitsukoshi organizer, whom I shall call B., was the son of a distinguished Italian art historian. His extreme political opinions having made him unwelcome in Fascist Italy, he had fled to Nazi Germany; there too he found himself unwelcome, so moved on to Tokyo. He married a Geisha, a painter of some repute, who died of tuberculosis when they were both interned in a Japanese concentration camp after the fall of Italy in 1944. Later he married another Geisha and became more traditionally Japanese than the Japanese themselves. He wore a kimono, and affected long nails and a wispy beard.

Before we travelled to Osaka, where the exhibition was to open, B. escorted me around Kyoto for two days, as a gesture of thanks. Having visited all the well-known pleasure pavilions on the tourist itinerary, I expressed a wish to see some smaller, private gardens. He was as interested as I was, and willingly drove me all around the outskirts of Kyoto. We found one decayed garden where the house had been demolished. Another cast took us down a narrow lane with high walls, protective of something. 'What's behind there?' I asked. He gave a non-committal shrug. 'But what's behind that door?' I demanded, pointing to a seventeenth-century entrance. We stopped. I got out and tried the latch. It opened. Shocked at this invasion of another's privacy, B. at first refused to leave the car. Then, without warning, he suddenly leapt out and rushed through the door, exclaiming with astonishment and joy, 'But this is where I spent my first honeymoon, in 1939!' The house or pavilion was in the traditional Japanese style, nineteenth-century in date. It was silent, shut up, and seemingly abandoned. The garden was in complete decay. A series of shaped pools completely covered with water-lilies extended from a ruined tea house of, I think, earlier date than the house. B. told me it had belonged to a nobleman. I walked about, but he sat by the tea house as if in a dream, wrapped up in his own thoughts. I was content to sit there too. We left a hour later for Tokyo, and next morning took the Bullet Train to Osaka.

I was accommodated in a Mitsukoshi hotel, and taken to the department store the following morning. The allotted space seemed far too large for my moderately sized exhibition. I was used to drawings being presented two or three feet apart; here, they were about six feet apart. Before that first day ended I had sworn never again to become involved with an exhibition in commercial premises. For all my contention that the technicalities of conservation can be over-done, illumination the density of arc lights was clearly unsuitable for Jones's delicate and precious drawings, and I nearly caused a diplomatic incident by refusing to exhibit them until proper environmental controls were put in place. The British trade representative and consular officials in Osaka were kept busy placating the Mitsukoshi top brass, but B. sympathized with my objections. I could not believe my eyes on the opening day: more than two thousand visitors poured through, but most looked neither to right nor left. For all they seemed to mean to most of them, Inigo Jones's drawings might just as well have been photographs by Cecil Beaton.

I hated Osaka and yearned to get on with the rest of my planned itinerary, a visit to the Chinese porcelain collections in Taipei and then on to India. I had still to endure a presentation by the Mitsukoshi managers. It was futile to hope that I might be allowed to choose a moderately useful gift from the store, but I dropped a hint to this effect to my Italian, and he to the managers. When the time came the ceremony was stiffly formal and notable for its interminable speeches. The managers lined up behind a long table, to one side of which were six white-coated young men. With fascinated horror I noted, under covers, a very large object indeed. Upon an incomprehensible (to me) command, two of the white-coated assistants reverently withdrew the cover, revealing a four and a half foot long *faux*-lacquer tube. Then the other four assistants leapt forward to extract from it and unroll a huge embroidered silk tablecloth of such awfulness as to defy description: black silk, highly embossed coloured embroidery and swirly ugly patterns linger in my memory. There was applause. I mumbled my thanks, my true thoughts inexpressible. My Italian had faded away, perhaps embarrassed by my behaviour. I fled to the hotel lugging the tube, happy that at least this Far Eastern farce was over. But it wasn't, quite.

I was to leave the next morning for Taipei. I dubiously eyed the lacquer tube, and also my heavy overcoat, which I would not need once I'd left the damp cold of Japan behind me. A pleasing thought occurred to me. On the way to the store I had crossed a bridge over a fast-flowing river. I waited until midnight, slipped surreptitiously out of the hotel, shiftily made my way to the bridge, peered around, and hastily unburdened myself of both tube and overcoat. They were swept away on the night currents. Back at the hotel I lay in bed and fantasized about possible headlines in the *Osaka Daily News*: 'Clothing and valuable Mitsukoshi present found in river. Suspected suicide of British organizer of Inigo Jones exhibition, following erratic behaviour and dispute.'

Some years later Eileen and I were eating in Savini's, in Milan's Galleria Vittorio Emanuele II, when who should I see coming towards us but my extremist Italian friend from Japan. He certainly saw me, he was there as I turned my head to speak to Eileen — but in those few seconds of distraction he disappeared, back to his twilight world.

38

Strange happenings at Ashcroft

IT ALL BEGAN with a telephone call in May 1973 from Jim Lees-Milne: 'We've just been to Joannie and Charlie Harford at Ashcroft. Alvilde gets her bedding plants from Bert Parsons there. There's a cottage, not fit for anyone but a pig – but the views! Uninterrupted to the Warminster Downs, thirty miles away.' Ashcroft House was a squire's demesne where the old kitchen garden was now a commercial nursery run by Bert, Doris and Valerie Parsons. The idea of a country bolt-hole was irresistible, so we took the cottage, although in winter the inner walls of a bathroom made of breeze-blocks were sheets of ice.

This is a tale of a secret, secluded part of England, known only to a few. The four Gloucestershire valleys of Ozleworth, Boxwell, Lasborough and Tyley form a triangle, the apex of which is the ruined medieval Calcot Barn where the A46 crosses the A4135, its base a line from Wotton-under-Edge to Alderley (where Jim lived). The deep valleys were formed by glaciers from the precipice of the Cotswold escarpment scouring down to debouch onto the flats of the Vale of Berkeley.

Our first walk in the steps of Jim Lees-Milne took us below

22. The Ozleworth Valley, Gloucestershire: where the white unicorn runs

Ozleworth Park towards the Boxwell Valley and the ancient decayed drive to the Huntleys' Boxwell Court, so hidden among box woods that in 1651, after the Battle of Worcester, Charles II and his companions were able to make their way to it undetected to pass one night with Captain Matthew Huntley. In a gesture that, repeated elsewhere, endeared him to antiquarians as yet unborn, Charles lopped off a lock of his hair before leaving. As might be expected, the four-poster bed in which he is said to have slept has been preserved. On a memorial in the tiny adjoining church with its thirteenth-century bellcote is a wistful inscription honouring the Huntleys, 'deeply oppressed by the adherence of their family to the failing fortunes of the Stuart Kings'.

But I digress. We are not in the Ozleworth Valley to seek the phantoms of the Stuarts, but to relate a curious incident. On this, our first foray into the valley, our eight-year-old son Lucian said, quite unprompted, 'There's been a big battle here.' A few weeks later there appeared in the local paper a report of a lecture in which a local historian put forward the theory that King Arthur had come out of Wales and crossed the Severn by the Roman fort at Arlingham to fight his last great battle around the vast Iron Age camp of Uley Bury, afterwards retreating to the Ozleworth valley. In the lane behind Newark Park is an old concrete, cor-rugated-iron-roofed Observation Post left over from the last war, when it was occupied twenty-four hours a day, spotting German planes flying overhead to Bristol. Bert Parsons was a fund of tales told him by his father, and one concerned an observer who was twice disturbed in the middle of the night by shouts and metal-lic clashes that sounded like swords. When he opened the door of the OP there was only an oppressive silence, unusual for high summer. So frightened was the observer that his report of this incident eventually found its way into the Public Record Office. I like the idea of these ghostly battles, and there may well have been more than one, for after all, in Arthur's day the nearby Roman military city of Chessalls, adjacent to Ashcroft, was probably still above ground, in ruins. In our time the old Observation Post still contained official notices and a broken telephone, together with an amplitude of used condoms amid strewn hay, evidence of its popularity as a trysting-place for Wootton's girls and boys.

In the Ozleworth valley the beech woods hang thick and pre-cipitous. Before the county's new mapping of the footpaths, this was always a place of solitude. Once, during the early months of what we liked to call 'our possession' of 'our valley', we glimpsed a white flash which we thought might be an animal passing through the trees. But it was too white for a deer. The spell the valley cast made it seem very reasonable for myth to become matter: we wondered if it might be a unicorn. Alas, not. As we later discovered, it was the writer and traveller Bruce Chatwin, naked but for his sandals. We glimpsed him thus several times, as did our son Lucian when he was among the fox holes, looking for fossils. Years later, he remembered the incident: 'His winky was very small.' Bruce lived lower down the valley, at Holwell Farm. Somehow he never responded to the magic and seclusion of the valley; he certainly never wrote about it, and disliked the shadows that cast Holwell into gloom. I recalled his white and naked purity when I saw him in his wheel-chair, so sadly emaciated with Aids.

This is ancient country, impregnated not just with the echoes but with the physical evidences of early man. We field-walked constantly in the course of our quarter of a century here, and discovered thousands of flint implements. The Chessalls may possibly have been one of the largest Roman military camps between Cirencester and Bath. On Eileen's second visit to shop in Wotton, she was stopped in the street by a dirty, gypsy-like old hag with a large strawberry mark across her face who said, 'You come from up there' – indicating with her hand the Ozleworth escarpment. ''Tis a coven of witches there.' At Newark Park, by coincidence, lived Bob Parsons – from Texas, no relation of Bert at Ashcroft. Newark is a hunting lodge in the Henrician taste. The genial Bob was there already when we arrived at Ashcroft, and would have readily subscribed to the presence of witches. Our daughter Georgina used to ride his huge slavering Great Danes, whose habit it was to bay at night, conspiring with the ghosts and phantoms in the house; we heard they once ate a small dog belonging to Elizabeth Chatwin. Poltergeists were reputed to be very active at Newark, and footsteps could be heard clattering up and down stairs at night. Lucian heard them – but wondered if they were not merely Bob's friends, hastening from one room to another. Jim Lees-Milne claimed that his whippets would whine outside and refuse to enter the house. The Poltergeist Society paid Newark a visit in 1968, but got so drunk that no amount of activity would have awoken them.

Bert, of the indigenous Parsonses, was full of extraordinary local details, and was convinced there had been poltergeists at Kingscote Park. The manor of Kingscote passed in family succession for eight hundred years until 1951, when the last Kingscote decamped in an alcoholic haze and the house was demolished. All very Irish, somehow. At the demolition sale Bert discovered a mountain of empty whisky and gin bottles in the attics. Don Parsons of Tetbury, Bert's cousin, a house-clearance dealer, bought some late seventeenth-century panelling that had been retained when the William and Mary house was rebuilt in the early nineteenth century. In 1947 the Poltergeist Society had spent a night in the room in which it had been installed. Strangely, Don Parsons could never sell it, and so he gave it to us, commenting, ''Tis tainted with ghosts.' A panel now hangs on the stairs of my house at Badminton: it has fallen off the wall four times.

Above Lasborough stands the disused church of Newington Bagpath. Here the vibes could not be nastier. The church sits on the site of a Roman temple, flanked by a motte and bailey earthwork, and commands the grassy outlines of a vanished village. It is abandoned and derelict, although according to the Church Commissioners it was sold nearly twenty-five years ago to an architect in Zambia. Bert recalled a strange theory connected with the church, handed down in his family. Sometime in the nineteenth century, a felon from Bagpath, waiting to go to the gallows in Stroud, prophesied that the church would become desecrated and ruined. When his body was taken down from the gallows, his family arranged for it to be conveyed to Bagpath for secret burial, hidden under hay in a cart. Three times on the journey from Stroud the corpse slipped out from under the hay, as if still alive. By the time he got to Hunter's Hall at Kingscote, the carter had had enough, and fled in terror. He was Bert Parsons' grandfather. From Hunter's Hall the body was carried to Newington Bagpath, where it was buried in an unmarked grave.

In 1965 we found the door of the church open. The church was no longer in use, and had been emptied of furniture and fittings, but on a shelf we spied a handsome yellow glazed jar. Furtively we removed it, and took it back to Ashcroft Garden Cottage, and filled it with flowers. On the third day there was a crash: the jar had burst asunder. God help the Zambian architect if he ever tries to live there.

39

Fiery Juhre

Aqualate Hall

IN THE 1970s Gervase Jackson-Stops was driving Eileen and me across England from Powis Castle in Wales to his Menagerie at Horton in Northamptonshire. As usual with Gervase at the wheel, stuttering at every obstruction, it was a manic drive, and as usual it was accompanied by what Ian Nairn described as Pevsner-bashing: the gleeful identification of buildings the 'Herr Doktor Professor' (*pace* Betjeman) had missed. What joy it was to know that he had missed so much – for had he not, there would have been nothing more to discover. As always on such travels, I was the map-reader.

Outside Market Drayton we had passed RAF Ternhill aerodrome when we noticed Buntingsdale Hall on the map. We knew it by repute: a grand red-brick baroque house designed by John Prince and built by Francis Smith about 1719. We would do a 'hit-and-run'. A faded War Department notice at the entrance to the approach warned against trespass and threatened prosecution. Disregarding it, we drove up to the forecourt area where we found an empty sentry-box and a wooden shed of the guard-room sort. The house was looming and large, wrapped around with giant pilasters, and with so many heavy keystones to the windows as to suggest an attack of architectural hiccups – or, as Gervase comically put it, 'No, it's me, stuttering.' There was an unnerving air of 'presence' about it, as if it were not quite as unoccupied as it looked. The windows were all dirty and blind. Was it RAF property, we wondered, peering through a window. It did seem to be abandoned, but even Gervase did not like the vibes, so we left, turning back onto the A41, the old Roman road to Newport, in a south-easterly direction. Two miles further along that road, with Ternhill aerodrome on our right, we were buzzed by a helicopter. Was it due to our intrusion at Buntingsdale? We knew not, but had a lot of fun wondering whether it might be one of those safe houses where MI6 kept spies, or tortured informants.

Just beyond Newport I noticed Aqualate Hall on the map, and gave a shriek. From books about John Nash I knew it had been a house in Tudoresque taste with exotic onion domes, designed in 1805 for Sir John Fletcher Boughey. Gervase told us that Sacheverell Sitwell had come this way in search of a fantasy house for a book he was writing, but found nothing. We turned to Pevsner's *Staffordshire*, and from his sparse description it was obvious he had never obtained access: 'Rebuilt after a fire in [November] 1910 by Walter Tapper,' he informed us. Eileen recalled that Mary Miller, of Chillington Hall in the same county, had once told her that her cousin Celina Juhre lived at Aqualate, a person of amiable disposition, but very inhospitable to trespassers. The omens were not auspicious.

First we encountered the anticipated park wall, and in it an unassuming side entrance bearing two of what proved to be many more notices of the sort Jane Austen would have described as 'repulsive': 'The dogs here are dangerous'. Ha, ha! *We* were safe in the car. A Georgian stable range with cupola appeared, perhaps, we thought hopefully, indicative of something surviving of the Nash house. Yet more notices: 'Keep Out', 'Beware of the Dogs'. A gap between two ranges, obviously leading to the house, seemed less than inviting in the circumstances. I was ordered out to reconnoitre. Peering furtively around a corner I glimpsed a courtyard and a gabled front, and an estate car. I retreated. Peering at the map, I concluded that if we went through one of the other gaps we could do a sweep through the park and exit by what seemed to be the lower lodge. It ought to give us a good view of the Tapper house. The park looked perfectly Reptonian, Aqualate Mere shimmered in the sun, the drive made a perfect curve, and at the appropriate moment Gervase leapt out quickly to snap the house. 'God,' he cried, 'what a boring architect Tapper was. Who would want to live there?' It looked a muddle from this distance, and we could not decide whether or not Nash had incorporated an earlier gabled house. Whoops! No time for such deliberations. We nipped back into the car, and set off along the drive to the exit.

A Picturesque Nash–Repton lodge with Tudoresque gates appeared. It seemed to be uninhabited; at any rate, there was no sign of an angry gate-keeper at what seemed to be the main gates. I got out to open them, and then uttered an imprecation: 'Gawd, they're padlocked.' Gervase turned the car round, and as he did so we noticed the estate car I had seen coming slowly but relentlessly towards us, the sound of barking dogs growing louder and louder. A door opened, black growling dogs leapt out, and our bonnets met, like lovers kissing. But this was no amorous conjunction. The slavering hounds lunged and barked, and out leapt a woman we took to be the chatelaine, Celina Juhre. So incandescent with rage was she that we later christened her Fiery Juhre of Aqualate. 'Damn you!' she bellowed. 'Can't you read the notices? Get out of here. I'll follow.'

We jinked around her car, and follow she did. Her car was right up the arse of ours, bonnet to exhaust. 'Wish cars could fart,' Gervase laughed. He deliberately drove very slowly. Fiery Juhre followed us, her hounds barking the while, not just to the stable range but onto the main road. We turned away and were waving with relief and bravado when Gervase suddenly stopped the car. Here was yet another entrance with an even prettier Nash–Repton Picturesque lodge, but in very poor condition (it was described in 1991 as 'now badly decaying'). Gervase got out to take a snap, determined to report it to the Georgian Group. With a squeal of brakes, there was Fiery Juhre again. For a brief moment it seemed as though Gervase's small frame would be annihilated by her expansive bulk. Then we heard his furious, stuttering voice: 'Fetch the police, then. This is a public road. I'm reporting this lodge to the Georgian Group.' She stepped back as though he had threatened to assault her: she had met her match.

We drove off, regretting that we had been unable to enlighten either her or ourselves with regard to her house, for as Pevsner might have said, 'Its architectural history needs elucidation'. We had just turned back on to the A41 when a police car sped by, heading from Newport, in the direction of Aqualate, apparent confirmation that she had indeed called the rozzers. When we reported all this to Mary Miller, she blanched. 'I'll have to disown you,' she said.

40

Aaahh! Aaahh!

Ilsington House

IN 1993 GERVASE Jackson-Stops, his friend Ian Kirby, Eileen and I were sweeping through Dorset on a country house and nursery-garden tour. We had Melbury House in view at the end of the day, and an appointment with Charlotte Morrison, the affable chatelaine there. Punctuality was demanded. As was our wont, we had made many 'hit-and-run' casts up the drives of houses along the way, alarming owners peering from windows, turning away fast if the house looked boring. Nearing Dorchester, we noticed in our *Historic Houses* guide a compelling description of Ilsington House at Puddletown, east of the town: 'William and Mary mansion . . . Home of George III's illegitimate grandson . . .' It was all too tantalizing. In the 'Buildings of England' *Dorset* volume Pevsner and John Newman were specific enough about the exterior but, from their description, seemed not to have been inside. 'Let's try it. Won't take more than half an hour,' said Gervase.

As we drew into the approach drive, we saw an enormously plump girl sitting inside the open back of a small van, her bum squashed on the edge. She sold tickets to the house but fumbled with the money, was not sure when the next tour was due, and had no guide for sale. It was attractively amateur. No matter. We had a little time in hand, and reckoned that a tour could not last more than twenty minutes. Very likely we would be allowed to walk through unattended. We wandered into the garden, intrigued by the claim that it had the longest ha-ha in the county. A nice friendly-looking country lady planting flowers was obviously the owner. We dismissed the ha-ha, for it was no longer than the one at Stowe Gardens, and guessed that a late seventeenth-century house had been refronted around 1720.

Time was passing. Looking apprehensively at our watches, we were relieved when a door opened and we were invited in. With us were seven other visitors, three women and four men. Ilsington is a plain William and Maryish sort of house of perhaps around 1710 with a hall of no particular distinction, much altered in the 1930s, opening up into the higher staircase space. We debated the true date of the stairs: probably William and Mary, we thought, but maybe Edwardian. However, it was the 'private collection of pictures' ranged on the walls that stunned us. They belonged to the very modern school, and in our fogyish eyes seemed inappropriate to their setting. Never mind, that was none of our business.

Then we were welcomed by a red-faced woman holding a thick sheaf of typescript. She was of the nice rural sort who are the mainstay of many a Women's Institute. To our concern, she began to read monotonously from her papers about the history of the house and its treasures, and ten minutes later was still reading. We shuffled, mumbled, exchanged despairing looks, gazed at the swirly paintings on the walls. Our fellow visitors seemed to lap it all up. In such moments of boredom the mind wanders, and seeks strange diversions. Gervase said later he had been wondering what would happen if we suddenly took off all our clothes and ran naked through the house. The architectural glories of the staircase could have been covered in two minutes, but took fifteen. Finally we ascended the stairs, not alas to pass into the next rooms but to receive yet another lengthy lecture at the top. 'My God!' we muttered to ourselves. Gervase was growing more and more upset, whispering 'Melbury' to himself and twitching his leg about in irritation, as stutterers often do. We were exasperated, too, by our humdrum fellow visitors, half asleep, their eyes glazed over, seemingly lapping up a lecture that droned on and on. How we longed to tell the dear lady that much of it was unnecessary.

At last we moved from the upper landing into the gallery or drawing room, so arranged as to look like a display of brown furniture and attendant objects in an auction room. 'This', we were told, 'is where the Prince Regent entertained his guests.' 'How can we get out of here?' moaned Gervase, now almost jumping up and down. Ian too was beginning to look desperate, longing I knew for the flowers in the garden. But the red-faced woman droned on and on.

Suddenly I had an idea: I would feign a heart attack. I made a sign to Gervase and Ian, and I thought Eileen too had caught my eye. 'Aaahh!' I moaned loudly, and again 'Aaahh!', holding my chest and doubling up as if in agony. 'I've forgotten my heart pills,' then, hoarsely, 'they're in the car. Quick, we must get them.' Gervase supporting me, to the alarm of the garrulous guide and the other visitors we rushed out of the room and down the stairs, subsiding in giggles at the bottom. But poor Eileen hadn't cottoned on to the ploy, it seemed. All but in tears, because she thought I was really ill, she shouted angrily: 'This is no laughing matter! For goodness' sake, phone for an ambulance.' After all, I did take pills daily for high blood pressure. Then the truth dawned, and she joined in our laughter. We made for the beckoning front door, but to our horror it was locked! Providentially I spied a key on a ledge. It turned, the door opened, and freedom was ours. We cavorted across the lawn like lunatics, overjoyed to be free of our droning guide. We were disgracefully late for the amiable Charlotte but Melbury was a happy experience of a quite different order.

41

The blind woman
and 'the Boy'

Fawley Court

O N 30 NOVEMBER 1983, Christie's were to sell a group of
architectural designs by John Freeman, the amateur archi-
tect-owner of Fawley Court near Henley. Fawley Court is a late
seventeenth-century house often attributed to Wren, improved
by Freeman in the 1730s, then improved again in 1770–1 by his
son Sambrook Freeman. Sambrook employed James Wyatt for
the interior decorations, and also commissioned him to design
the Island Temple, familiar landmark of the Henley Regatta.

Among the drawings was Wyatt's design for the temple's interior, in an Etruscan-Grotesque style. The date of the actual decoration is not precisely known, but is perhaps *c.* 1772, which
would make it one of the first examples in England of this
Etruscan style, practised also by Robert Adam. Eileen and I
knew of the Temple, although we had never visited it, so we
encouraged Robin Griffith-Jones of Christie's British Drawings
Department to take us there to compare Wyatt's design with the
decorations *in situ*. Uncertain who owned the Temple, or how
to obtain access, we planned to call first upon the Polish Fathers
at Fawley Court, a seminary since before the last war.

The good Fathers were most solicitous to help. We toured the house and admired a number of antique Roman marbles from the famous Arundel Collection, bought by a Freeman in the seventeenth century, but found the banal new buildings in the grounds regrettable. John Freeman's follies and garden buildings survived, but alas we did not recognize the ancient Roman marble from Pergamum incorporated as a decorative feature in one of them: that was a later discovery by a fortunate archaeologist. When we enquired about the ownership of Temple Island, we found it belonged to 'old blind Mrs Mackenzie', a member of the railway baron family who had bought Fawley from the Freemans in the 1880s, and who still lived in Fawley village.

Our first stop was the Freeman mausoleum in Fawley churchyard. In 1748 John Freeman refitted the interior of the church using furniture from the dismantled chapel at the Duke of Chandos's Cannons House at Edgware, and in 1750 he built the neo-Roman mausoleum, where he was buried in 1752. We walked to the village for a ploughman's lunch in the local pub, and the publican gave us directions to 'old blind Mrs Mackenzie'. Behind a high hawthorn hedge pierced by a broken wooden gate and across a densely overgrown garden we glimpsed a half-timbered Edwardian cottage with an open front door beckoning. We knocked, and waited. No reply. We ventured to call out her name. This resulted in a shuffle-shuffle, tap-tap, and then a high-pitched voice exclaimed, 'Who is there?' Mrs Mackenzie was very old and crinkly of face, bowed and blind, but possessed of abundant mental energy and alertness. In the friendliest manner she said, 'Come in. Tell me who you are. I sense three of you.' We were led into a low sitting room containing leftovers from Fawley: a decent Gaspardesque picture, some Freeman furniture, and objects of Mackenzie Victorian taste. Alas, we did not see the wooden box which held the contents of a spoof barrow John

Freeman had constructed and filled in the 1730s: he was an ardent antiquarian, a member of the Society of Dilettanti and a Director of the East India Company. After Mrs Mackenzie's death this curiosity was bought at the sale of her effects by Christopher Gibbs, who gave it to the museum in Henley.

'Of course you can see the Temple,' she said, 'and then come back here for tea. I'll call the Boy.' Robin excitedly produced the Wyatt drawing for Mrs Mackenzie to see, then realized his *faux-pas*. What followed was extraordinary: she asked Robin to describe every detail and colour of the drawing, and as he did so, she commented upon what she remembered of the decorations in the Temple. She had been blind for many years, yet as we were soon able to confirm, she was right in every particular.

We wondered about 'the Boy', with whom we were to rendezvous on the Berkshire towpath, beyond the Regatta buildings. Sure enough, there he was waiting for us, smiling under a mop of tousled ginger hair. We supposed he was a Boy Scout, and he looked one, except that he was boss-eyed, with a twitch. He had the keys to the Temple, and to the padlock of the boat. That boat . . . it was full of rainwater. But 'the Boy', undeterred, leapt in (up to his knees), fished out a jug and began to bail vigorously. We warily surveyed the brown swirling water between the bank and the island; it was late October and the river was high. We were not cheered by the information that the boat had nearly foundered when Mrs Mackenzie had her seventy-fifth birthday party on the island. As we gingerly boarded it rocked and took in water, and to our alarm a squirt of Thames appeared through a crack in the stern. Nevertheless, we shoved off, Robin and I bailing away like mad, 'the Boy' rowing. Eileen moaned gently as she observed that the water coming in alarmingly exceeded the water being jugged out. However, she was a champion swimmer: Robin was not, and I am only average. Before we reached the island we were soaked to the knees. 'The Boy' was unconcerned, unlike Robin, now muttering in trepidation about Christie's, and the precious Wyatt drawing, and what would he do if the boat sank with it? It did not, the island was reached, the boat was moored, 'the Boy' carried on bailing, and we three squelched about examining the Temple. It was octagonal, a little reminiscent of a neo-Greek monument. Inside, a banqueting room faced upriver towards Henley and its bridge. There were the tall panels of Etruscan-style decoration, just as Wyatt had suggested in his drawing. If it had indeed been designed in 1773, Eileen observed, it pre-dated Robert Adam's Etruscan Room at Osterley.

We became concerned for Robin's sanity as he looked out of the Temple window and bewailed the expanse of water to be crossed once again. In the kitchen of the Temple I found a saucepan and commandeered it, so that two of us could bail while 'the Boy' rowed. This improved matters, but not even 'the Boy' could row against a strong current and a cutting breeze. So instead of attempting to fight the current he allowed the boat to be taken a few hundred yards downriver, where we muddily clambered up the bank. 'Let's get back to London,' Robin suggested urgently. We concurred, and sent 'old blind Mrs Mackenzie' our apologies via 'the Boy'. Eileen and I later wondered whether this incident had anything to do with Robin's decision to leave Christie's and take Holy Orders.

42

Buzz, buzz, little girls beware

Opočno

IN THE SUMMER of 1990 plans were afoot for an unofficial 'British Conservation Group' to be let loose in Czecho-slovakia. The Group was to comprise Gervase Jackson-Stops of the National Trust, Jonathan Bourne, a distinguished authority on French furniture, Reinier Baarsen, Chief of Decorative Arts at the Rijksmuseum, Lavinia Davies, of Kabul and, more recently, Istanbul, and of course Eileen and me. Confronted with the then intractable accommodation problem in Prague, and despairing of finding a hotel, Gervase had boldly asked his friend in the Foreign Office to help: through him, we were converted into an *official* British Conservation Group – or, rather, into the 'UK Working Party On Historic Houses and Castles in Czechoslovakia'. Moravia and Bohemia were now ours to command.

The poor denizens of the old Austro-Hungarian Empire have never recovered from the experience. Whenever a castle or country house came into sight, especially if it was empty or in ruins, as so many are, it was under the barbed wire with us, up, over and in, hoisting ourselves through windows. Curators of

23. The British Conservation Group on view at Troja, near Prague, 1990

well-preserved historic properties still dubiously recall the laughter and idiosyncratic behaviour that went hand-in-hand with a demonstration of unsurpassed scholarly examination and criticism. Indeed, this visit laid the basis for SAVE Europe's Heritage initiatives with regard to the problems facing Czech castles and country houses. We computed that in Moravia and Bohemia alone there are at least 12,600 castles, country houses, and what are called 'towers', often just a pile of stones. We reckoned the situation was comparable to that in Britain after the Second World War, when in 1955 alone, for example, one substantial historic house was demolished every two days or so.

We were given the special privilege of a private tour with a personal guide, during which in theory all doors were willingly opened. But in 1990 much of the old Communist way of thinking survived in pockets of resistance. We took a strong aversion to some curators, not least the one at Opočno. He was surly and

24. Opočno: the Gallery Courtyard

uncommunicative, a Communist diehard. Despite telephone calls from his boss in Prague instructing him to allow us to study the house at our leisure, he would have none of it, and made us conform to the public tour. We were commanded in a stentorian voice to wait on wooden benches in that glorious north-Italianate sixteenth-century galleried courtyard, where other prospective visitors were literally standing to attention, waiting for the next tour to begin in about half an hour. Our own kindly guide was embarrassed, and whispered that if we would wait for twenty minutes or so in the gardens, she would see to it that we had the access we required.

As was the case with so many renaissance castles in the Austro-Hungarian Empire, the old geometrical formal gardens

25. Opočno: showing exact location of the wasp incident on
lower terrace

had long since been replaced by a landscape park in what was always described as the 'English style', which invariably meant grass up to the windows and a selection of follies. These early nineteenth-century Czech parks are among the loveliest in Europe, and Opočno was no exception, landscaped along a ravine, the Valley of the Golden Brook, with several informal lakes and a sinuous walk. Along this walk, which was open to the public, we decided to take a stroll, to examine a beautiful greenhouse. It was a balmy early evening, the warm sun gently sinking at the end of a satisfactory day in which we had crossed a total of eleven houses off our list. We sauntered contentedly in the company of a number of local people also enjoying the balmy evening. Suddenly I felt a movement in my trousers, accompanied by an angry buzzing as I was stung on my inner thigh by a wasp. I uttered a yell, and a friend of my attacker also struck. More yells.

In the circumstances, what *could* I have done but drop my trousers to release my assailants? There was I on the public path, semi-naked, trousers on the ground, showing my silk knickers, when to my alarm what should I see approaching but two pretty flaxen-haired little girls dressed in gingham frocks, strolling arm-in-arm. They stopped and stared, transfixed by this unexpected barrier to their passage, then cried out and clasped one another tightly in horror. They froze. Not speaking their language, what could I do to explain my predicament but resort to sign language, first flapping my arms to demonstrate the flight of a wasp, then loudly droning a realistic 'buzz-buzz, buzz-buzz, buzz-buzz' through my teeth? The girls blenched, then screamed and ran wildly up to the castle. Reinier blenched, too. 'Oh my God,' he moaned, seeing the makings of an international incident and his job at the Rijksmuseum in jeopardy. The wasps, like the girls, had fled, so I hauled up my trousers and was hustled back to the courtyard.

Here the hard-line Commie curator instructed us in a severe tone to sit on the benches, where we received a monotonous half-hour harangue, in Czech of course. Our guide attempted to translate for us, but got a frosty stare. Nevertheless, we all concluded that, in view of the 'buzz-buzz' incident, it was safer for the British Conservation Group to be inside. We found the interiors had suffered from the installation of crude French-style decorations before the First World War: there were not many signs of the renaissance interiors that must at one time have complemented the beautiful courtyard. Worth all our tribulations, however, was the Armory containing the Collorado-Mansfeld Collection with its superb Milanese pieces, one of the great national treasures of the country. As we left we grumbled because the curator had refused to open up two public rooms containing the most important pictures; we were also horrified that the eighteenth-century pavilions by the architect Alliprandi had been painted a garish red and white. I think our tour guide was afraid we would make a scene with the curator, or feared the parents of the girls who had been buzzed might have called the police, for she hurriedly bundled us into the bus and drove off very fast.

43

Hořín and the Hurricane pilot

Among our visits to country houses during our first tour of Czechoslovakia in 1990 was an impromptu one to Hořín, at Melnik, not far from Prague. We had been told to expect a Lobkowicz family castle, built around 1700 by Alliprandi and Kanka but reconstructed by the baroque architect Johann Christian Spannbrucker from 1736 to 1746. It was currently said to house Polish agricultural workers, but was soon to be returned to Prince George Lobkowicz. Our car bumped up a muddy road to a gated screen across the *cour d'honneur*. It was like a theatrical setting, for the buildings enclosing the courtyard – the stable, chapel and service quarters – made an oval in a square, imparting movement. On the 'stage' were sheds, piles of rotting wood and timber, a line-up of dustbins, and six or seven grubby men sitting about, smoking. Then our eyes focused upon the iron scaffolding that concealed Spannbrucker's lively baroque façades. The metal was heavily rusted, so much so that one bit of scaffolding seemed to melt into another. How long had it been there, we wondered. As we stood there a little uncertainly, aware of our trespass, the men began to disperse, muttering to one another, presumably in Polish.

26. Hořín, Melnik, Prague: the discovery of the Hurricane
pilot, 1990

We walked warily around the outside of the house, still
puzzled by the rusted scaffolding. A coil of barbed-wire lay
across the stairs to the main entrance, so this was clearly not the
approach now in use. Oddly, the Poles had just melted away –
but where to? A side door in the rear of a wing yielded to
Gervase's shoulder, the lock broken: this must be the usual way
in, for the regular and recent tread of feet through at least an
inch of hardened mud had worn a track along the floor of the
passage. Cream paint was everywhere. If the people working
on it had abandoned the house, it could not have been long
ago. A few rooms possessed benches and tables, and in one
there was a blackboard, but there was nothing more. A grand
stone hall, probably by Alliprandi, had simple baroque mould-
ings, but they were hard to see as the windows were shuttered.

27. The Library, Hořín: desuetude of 1990

'This is a bit dull,' we thought – an understatement, if ever there was one.

Just as Gervase was beginning to become irritated, muttering and stuttering about breaking open an inner door, footsteps from the way we had come in made us turn, to see a Pole in greasy blue denims, possibly in his late sixties, and distinguished by a bushy moustache. Instead of more incomprehensible Polish, we were confounded by heavily accented but respectable English. He introduced himself with a name that sounded like Jerzy Jackowska, and told us his sad story: he had flown Hurricanes in a Polish squadron in the Battle of Britain, had met a Czech girl in London and followed her back to her family near Prague, where they were both trapped when the Russians invaded. He then explained about the Poles loitering in the courtyard. It was extraordinary. They were not farm workers, but builders. The

28. Gervase Jackson–Stops at Hořín, 1990

scaffolding had gone up in 1973, to mend the roof, and for seventeen years they had loitered on, being paid, the scaffolding proof that they were needed here. It was not unlike the farm co-operatives, Jerzy explained, where labourers were allocated not by need but by acreage, and paid irrespective of whether any job was completed. There was no incentive to work. He was aware of the possible return of Prince Lobkowicz from nearby Melnik. We were about to say goodbye when he asked, 'But have you seen the Stone Rooms?' We had not, and did not know what he meant.

He then disappeared, and in his place came a female caretaker with a key. This opened a quite insignificant door that led down from the *piano nobile* to a ground-floor suite of miraculous rococo rooms, among them a *sala terrana*. Gervase's later researches revealed that the stoves and the giant faience urns were by Joseph Zung and the frescos all by the Prague painter Ondrej Pacina, while the somewhat later but still wondrous white-and-gold library and alcove bedroom had been painted and gilded by Josef Dittman. We first gaped, then yelped with delight as we worked our way through the rooms. The decay was tragic – we could *smell* the huge dry-rot spores that simply oozed out of the woodwork – yet none of the painted lilacs, yellows, pinks and greens had ever been touched or restored. Not a lick of new paint, and no evidence of later cleaning. The bedchamber, with the bed alcove and the closet at the side, still with its close-stool, was an astonishing and rare survival. Jonathan Bourne sat himself down on the close-stool and refused to budge, unfairly and improperly cursing Prince Lobkowicz for possessing such a desirable house. We were unanimous: of all the rococo-decorated suites of rooms in Europe, *this* was the one we would all most want to live in, or take away with us.

44

A disturbance at Hewell Grange

WHEN NIKOLAS PEVSNER and Sandra Wedgwood visited Hewell Grange in 1966–7 for the 'Buildings of England' *Worcestershire* volume, the neighbouring towns of Redditch and Bromsgrove each covered no more than two square miles of urban growth and between them the countryside was still unspoiled. This was thanks to Hewell Grange itself, for the spreading estate nearly touches the perimeter of either town, as is nicely shown on the 1967 edition of the one inch to the mile Ordnance Survey map. Here you will find Hewell labelled 'HM Prison' and 'Brockhill Remand Centre', reminders that the Home Office bought the estate from the Earl of Plymouth in 1946. It seems likely that in doing so, it prevented the union of these two sprawling satellites of Birmingham.

Great changes have more recently occurred with regard to the roads hereabouts. Minor ones serving Hewell Grange have been bypassed, resulting in the isolation of two neo–classical entrance lodges designed for the sixth Earl of Plymouth by Thomas Cundy in 1815. They once flanked a drive that veered left to finish beneath the huge *porte-cochère* portico that Cundy added to what is known as the 'old house', built for the second Earl by Francis Smith of Warwick in 1712. Its shell, gutted since 1890 and completely shrouded in ivy, stands as a spectacular folly in the park. Today this old drive leads to the modern buildings of the prison, whereas a 'new' drive laid out in 1890 veers to the right and leads to a quite different architectural experience: the pink sandstone exuberance that is the Victorian Hewell Grange, designed by G.F. Bodley and Thomas Garner in 1884–91 for the 14th Baron Windsor (the earldom of Plymouth having fallen into abeyance) and his wife.

This is a bizarre tale of a group experience. In 1994 Eileen and I, John Martin Robinson, Tim Knox and Todd Longstaffe-Gowan bowled along the 1890 drive to be duly overwhelmed by the visual impact of this vast English Jacobean-style Victorian house with its many mullioned windows, built for one of the richest families in the land. Sweeping into the forecourt, nego-tiating a central island upon which, on a pedestal, stood an anguished 'Dying Gaul' in Croggan's artificial stone, we could well imagine the faces of inmates at the upper windows to be those of servants awaiting our commands. At the entrance, however, we found neither old-fashioned servitude nor gracious nobility to welcome us: the Home Office enquiry desk was plain and uninviting. But appearances are so often deceptive, for we were delivered into the interested care of Senior Officer John Gumley, intelligent historian of the place and our deputed guide this day.

As if the stupendous façade were not enough, we were totally unprepared for the vast scale of the longitudinal space of the hall, and the change in style from English Jacobean to early Italian renaissance. The contrast was made even more pointed by the exceptional richness of all the materials (the Chapel had a floor of lapis lazuli and was ceiled with cedar) and the presence of inmates playing snooker – scowling youths wearing shell-suits in the very place where The Souls once conversed, and probably played games with balls and cues on green baize too, but billiards rather than snooker.

The Plymouths (the earldom was revised in 1905) had left many of the fine fittings, works of art and furnishings in the house, on loan. One spectacular object forming the *point-de-vue* from the entrance magnetically drew our covetous gaze: a life-size bronze statue of Hermes standing on a pedestal in the screened recess of the smaller transverse garden hall. Was it late renaissance, we wondered, or maybe a rare neo-classical copy 'after the Antique', the masterpiece of Zoffali? It had been displayed by the Plymouths as if in a treasure chest, for the walls of this small hall were papered with *trompe-l'œil* painted tapestry, and the Italianate door-cases of variegated marbles increased the richness of the effect. My camera went snap snap, for we intended to seek the opinion of that great Roman scholar, Alvar Gonzales Palacios.

So obviously caring were the staff, so immaculate the upkeep, that we had constantly to remind ourselves that this was a prison. Somehow we expected Lord and Lady Plymouth to burst through a door at any moment to greet us. We yearned for a situation in which we could all be inmates of this glorious house! The glories extended outside, to the vast and immaculately maintained Italianate formal garden, a geometry of beds and topiary made by the gardener Andrew Pettigrew in the 1890s. As we emerged from the long vista of the garden we looked up, and there before us was the portico of the Riding School. Had we been transported to St Petersburg, we wondered – for the original brick red, mauvish and white colours of the painted exterior conveyed a distinctly Russian flavour. The raised caryatid portico, copied from the Erechtheum in Athens, was originally

29. Bronze statue of Hermes: Hewell Grange, Worcestershire
(Country Life)

a place from which to view what had been a semi-formal land-scape garden designed by Humphry Repton for the earlier house. Behind it was a wire fence, and behind that we discovered the ruined shell of the old Smith of Warwick house. We made our way over the wire and ran towards it in glee. Inside all was dank and smelly, the space resounding to the cooing of the hundreds of doves that dwelt here.

As we left the old ruined house to circle round again towards the forecourt of the new one we debouched into a contrived dell, and found ourselves in a grotto garden, probably by Repton. Most notable was the 'Palaeolithic' or 'Druidic' entrance, in the form of a giant boulder that swung on a pivot. My camera clicked and clicked. Then – disaster! I knew I had had a 24-exposure film in it, and here it was, registering 32 on the counter. Something was very wrong. It seemed all too likely that all the photographs I'd taken in the house were ruined, so once more we had to rendezvous with Hermes.

As the Enquiry Office Mr Gumley reassured us – 'No problem, just go in and take what you like. You know your way around' – and left us. But a different scene was now set before us. There were tables doubled along the length of the hall, and a hundred or so inmates were at dinner, before being confined to their rooms. As we crossed the hall we were conscious of being stared at. There was a slight murmur, which we ignored. Our destination was Hermes. I began to photograph the statue from various angles, snapping details of the legs, head, chest, buttocks and balls of this refined and burnished bronze. Then we were startled by the sound of a metal plate being tapped upon, then another, then more. The tapping grew louder and more insistent as the surly boys showed their displeasure. Others, evidently anxious to evade the camera's lens, fled, throwing their trays, plates and utensils to the ground. We were frightened. We had started a riot! A red-faced warder came running up, angrily shouting: 'I must ask you to leave immediately. Go, you are disturbing the men.' As the clattering became truly terrifying, more warders arrived. We hurtled through the entrance door. Gasping in the free air, we wondered: Did they think our photographs might reveal to unsuspecting parents or girlfriends that a favourite son or demon lover was *not* after all working hard at a holiday job in Spain?

45

The disciplinarian

Coughton Court

COUGHTON COURT IN Warwickshire, famous for the Throck-mortons, Catholic masses and the Gunpowder Plot, and now in the care of the National Trust, seemed an enticing stop on a Bank Holiday Sunday in 1994. We – Tim, Todd, Eileen and I – were disappointed to find a sign informing us that entrance was by timed ticket only. Ours was slated for one o'clock, so we went off to look at the two churches. On the way we passed the gatehouse to the Court, its door firmly closed and a queue winding away from it. Those waiting seemed ominously unsettled.

First we examined the parish church of St Peter, making a bee-line for the Tudor Throckmorton tombs. We particularly noted Sir Robert Throckmorton's grand tomb chest. He never occupied it, because he died in the Holy Land in 1518; instead it houses a later Sir Robert, who died in 1791. It seemed odd to have the Roman Catholic church of St Peter, St Paul and St Elizabeth built next door. As might have been expected of a church built for a deeply religious Catholic family, its architect in 1857 was J.A. Hansom, and there were good stained-glass windows by Hardman & Co.

It was time now to see the Court. Returning from the churches, I remarked that the people in the queue looked the same, but the queue was longer. About forty were now waiting. We joined what was obviously a very disgruntled group of people. The door of the gatehouse was ajar, and from inside could be heard a heated argument. As I love confrontations, I poked my head through the door. Half a dozen elderly visitors were in dispute with a young lady attendant at the desk. Their tickets were timed for 12.30, so why were they still being refused admission forty minutes later? To one side, barring the way through to the house, I observed a man and woman fiercely denouncing an authoritarian lady whom I shall call the Wardress. She was of an attractive rotund configuration that would have pleased those who like pneumatic bliss. In all my years of country-house visiting, never have I witnessed such adversarial domination by any guide in a house open to the public. While dealing with the denunciatory couple she also quelled the riotous grannies and issued staccato orders to the more placid aspirants in the queue: 'Keep in line . . . Don't lean on the barrier . . . It is dangerous to have too many visitors in the rooms at one time.' A meek-looking man had the temerity to ask, 'Surely, it doesn't take three-quarters of an hour for those inside to pass through?' The Wardress rounded on the rebel: 'That's my business. I decide when access shall be permitted.' I could think of certain friends who would have loved such discipline.

It was now half-past one, and half a dozen of those waiting in front of us had given up and gone away. The long queue was beginning to move, and we were happy. Now it was my turn to face the Mistress of the Entrance. She suddenly stopped the queue. I remonstrated with her. She was adamant. I grew choleric, and ever redder in the face. She threatened to 'fetch the police'. 'Do so!' I retorted. Eileen, Tim and Todd were cowering in the background. She was a mighty barricade, and I must confess I felt a hint of admiration. Then, as if aware that events were getting out of hand, she became subdued, moved aside, opened the door, and simply evaporated. We passed into the house unimpeded. I swear that never were there more than eight to ten visitors in any of the rooms. We all thought the place too contrived, obviously done over to create a more convincing 'ye olde' effect in the nineteenth century, when the Throckmortons brought the staircase, panelling and much else from their eighteenth-century seat at Harvington Hall in Worcestershire. It was all too sanitized, too *fumigated*. 'Give it back to the Throckmortons' was our opinion.

Tim told this tale to Gervase Jackson-Stops, and that mischievous and lovable friend played a joke on me two days later from his hospital bed. As 'Sergeant Jones' of the Redditch Constabulary, he telephoned me to follow up a complaint of affray laid by Lady Throckmorton, chatelaine of Coughton Court: at the least, I was likely to be charged with insulting behaviour. For a brief moment, I was taken in.

46

A chinoiserie adventure

Huish Park

FIRST LET ME describe the glimpse I had in the later 1940s of Coombe End House in Somerset, later to be renamed Huish Park. I had been bicycling (on my precious Claude Butler) in north Devon and Exmoor. Coombe End is in remote Heydon Hill country, full of tortuous lanes and secret coombs at their most rural, and few topographers have managed to do justice to the myriad of small worthwhile farmhouses and manors hereabouts. One such was Coombe End House, the focus of a tiny secluded valley. I remember it as a white house, large but quite plain, commanding one long view. It cast a spell over me, and much later I thought the house in R.F. Delderfield's *A Horseman Riding By*, then a favourite novel of my young daughter Georgina, must have been like Coombe End House. It was also reminiscent of a deserted mansion of the Irish Ascendancy.

The circumstances leading up to my second visit began at Francis Watson's death in 1992. Eileen and I had long enjoyed Francis's country retreats, which we often shared with him: the cottage in the Quantocks or the School House at Combe in Berkshire – but not the one at Corton in the Wylye Valley in

Wiltshire. By then Francis had adopted Ch'eng Yuan as his son and, by association, Ch'eng's friend the affable Graham Wild. Ch'eng had become a brilliant barrister in Hong Kong and Graham had distinguished himself there, launching the *South East Asian Review,* and when they were not in Hong Kong they were at Corton. Visitors to Corton before Francis's death must have been astonished by Ch'eng's Buddhist shrine with laquered walls, an altar, prayer mats and all the regalia. I never actually saw Francis on his knees there, but he was fond of telling all and sundry that it had been blessed by the Dalai Lama. At Corton Francis arranged his exquisite collection of drawings, bronzes, terracottas, porcelain, and divers pretty objects, all of which were left to Ch'eng – all except his library, already given to his friend Bobbie from the Ohio potato fields, who immediately sold it on to the Getty Museum. This, rightly, had enraged Ch'eng.

Eventually we heard that Corton had been sold and that Ch'eng and Graham had bought Coombe End House, which they re-christened Huish Park. Having heard so many bizarre tales of Francis and his *ménage,* it was natural that we should want to visit Huish. So out came the maps and off we set. 'Just down the M5 and off at Taunton, then A361 to Wiveliscombe,' said Tim Knox. It all seemed simple enough. We phoned, and Graham replied warmly, 'Of course, come. I'll call Ch'eng.' Ch'eng sounded a little cautious – 'But Graham's mum's here' – but in the end he amicably caved in to our pleas. 'Come, then. Lunch at one.' He gave me some directions, and hung up.

Possibly we should have dressed for the event in chinoiserie style but, exceptionally, the day promised to be a hot one, so we were lightly dressed, in pale colours. All went well as far as Taunton and Wiveliscombe; then things began to go desperately wrong (I had of course mislaid the directions). We drove along narrow lanes from Wiveliscombe to Maundown and to Huish

Champflower – but no Huish Park. One yokel we asked said, 'Never 'eard of Huish Park.' Had we come to the wrong Huish, we wondered? There was a Huish Barton in the county. We drove about aimlessly, through Clatworthy and past a huge reservoir. No Huish Park. We found ourselves at Huish Moor, but again of Huish Park not a sign. It was now time for lunch.

At Catford Winters was a sign to Coombe End. 'Aha!' I exclaimed: I remembered writing 'Coombe End' on my lost piece of paper. 'You're always throwing away important bits of paper,' complained Eileen. But where was Huish Park? A narrow muddy rutted track didn't really look like a drive, but we took it anyway. It turned out to be a cul-de-sac leading to a farm cottage, out of which shot a suspicious farmer. At our enquiry for Huish Park, he gave a loud guffaw. 'Huish Park? Ha! You mean Coombe End House. That's its proper name. Them Chiney peoples changed it to Huish Park. Back to the road, turn left, sign's on the left.' We were now late, but the goblin of the little lost piece of paper was about to wreak its full vengeance. A tractor approached along the track. Todd, who was driving, moved over onto the verge to make way. What *politesse*. What a mistake. The tractor drove on, our wheels sank into a ditch. Revving was useless, so out we tumbled, into the mud: mud on our shoes, mud up our pant-legs, mud all over our hands. Mud everywhere. By the time we had put down branches to give the tires grip, we were spattered with mud from top to toe. Then came my final undoing: I tripped on a root, lost my balance, and landed spread-eagled and face down in the ditch. I rose to shrieks of laughter. It was now two o'clock – but there, to our relief, was the sign, a spanking new one in stone with 'Huish Park' inscribed on it in gilt letters.

This was hardly the Coombe End House I had once seen from afar. Or at least, it was, but it was now all clean, with bright paint and new windows, the garden with close-cut verges. Bedraggled and be-muddied, we banged on the brassy new knocker. The door was opened by Ch'eng, at first smiling a joyful greeting, his smile then freezing as he took in our disgraceful muddy appearance, like stigs in the dump. His usually impassive Oriental face clouded over with an expression of horror. It wasn't just that we were an hour late: the whole place was squeaky clean. That was their way.

'Come in, come in,' cried Ch'eng, his habitual courtesy reasserting itself as he regained his composure. 'Does anyone want to use the bathroom?' he inquired hopefully; then, rather more forcefully, 'Perhaps you would like to slip out of those muddy shoes?' We complied gracefully, and padded into the lounge. Tim's socks had big holes in them, and one of Eileen's silk socks had torn right across, exposing all her muddied toes.

We were dispatched to various bathrooms. What must the spirits of the old Coombe End House have thought of all this plumbing? Each master bedroom possessed its own lavish bathroom. There were gold taps galore, exercise equipment, deep pile rugs for cavorting on, big mirrors to reflect naked bodies. We were exhorted to hurry up, and come and meet Graham's mum (it was now half-past two). As we passed through the rooms, we nearly fainted in the excessive central heating.

Entering the drawing room, we could scarcely believe what had happened to Francis's collection, so perfectly displayed at Corton. It was a travesty of presentation, in which his wonderful and rare objects had somehow lost their identity. The dark varnished Edwardian woodwork and heavy dark furniture induced an oppressive sense of gloom. Our eyes were distracted from one of Francis's notable treasures – a glittering ormolu clock depicting Charles X's coronation – by the bizarre sight of Graham's mum propped up on the sofa, apparently wrapped in a purple bath towel with bright yellow sunflowers, and wearing a white plastic shower cap. Her head nodded up and down, her rouged lips smiled and she dribbled a welcome, but the words that came mumbling out sounded like, 'Have the dustmen arrived?'

Two lithe and exquisite Chinese boys, polite and silent, produced and served a delicious lunch, which if not quite an early dinner was nearly a high tea. The conversation, naturally, was about Francis, in particular about his friend the potato boy from Ohio, who (Francis always said) had got in to Princeton as a Native American, under the new fad for positive discrimination, had submitted articles actually written by Francis, and successfully claimed five thousand dollars from Francis for graduating, when in fact he had failed his exams. Ch'eng hissed over this recollection.

Once we had eaten, we were enrolled as advisors in the placement of objects. On one sofa sat a huddle of gilded rococo wall brackets. 'I want to ask John and Eileen,' said Ch'eng, 'where shall these go? Here?' – he grasped one and held it above a door – 'Or there?' – holding it above a nearby girandole of gaudy ugliness – 'Or here?' – racing across the room and posing it above a picture. We all nodded.

Later on, we were interrupted in our tour of the house by the sound of a car drawing up on the gravel sweep outside. Who could it be? Graham hesitated on the landing, but the slender horde of beautiful boys had rushed to open the door and were calling up, 'Come Graham, come Graham, it is the Gwandmuvver cwok. The Gwandmuvver cwok has arrived.' We all ambled down, in some trepidation, to inspect the new arrival, and were soon dragooned into helping to lift it out of the car. The heavily French-polished horror was borne into the house. The smell of fresh sawdust and varnish was overpowering, its

226

recent construction barely disguised by layers of treacly varnish striving vainly to imitate old oak, the brassy eagle on its broken pediment more like a bonnet mascot on a new car. The horrid thing was placed in the hall, unhappy neighbour to an exquisite Louis Seize ormolu wall light. The graceful sloe-eyed lovelies danced around it admiringly.

It was time to go. We made our excuses and fled. We never could understand why Ch'eng and Graham had chosen the house. It has now been sold and they have moved on, we know not where. Perhaps we misbehaved so atrociously that they no longer want to know us. I hope 'Huish Park' has reverted to its old name, Coombe End House.

Indebtedness

IN THIS PRESENT excavation of memory I have been helped in many ways by vintage Snoopers such as Derek Sherborn, Desmond Fitz-Gerald, and Christopher Gibbs; and by younger ones, most notably Tim Knox and Todd Longstaffe-Gowan, both of whom have driven Eileen and me about as Companion Snoopers, playing the role of the late Gervase Jackson-Stops. I warmly thank those from whom I have made enquiries and received help: Neil Bingham, Sir Howard Colvin, Eric Degg, Kathy Demsky, Keith Farr, Sir William Gibbons, Ida Haugsted, Ian Jenkins, James Methuen-Campbell, James and Mary Miller, Meta Molstesen, Teresa Morales, Derek Pope, Peter Reid, Bill Rieder, Barbara Shapiro Comte, Willis van Devanter, David Watkin, Gloria Williams, Wim de Wit, and Christopher Woodward. Special thanks go to Eileen, who has been a support, and to Julian and Isobel Bannerman as guardians of the papers of Madame Vicaire. I salute my publisher John Murray, and my editor Liz Robinson, who described herself as 'hateful and interfering'. How right she is, how necessary for me as an author, and how beneficial have been her guidance and judgements. No author could owe his editor a greater debt.

Index

Index